RUNABOUTS
AND
ROADSTERS

RUNABOUTS
AND
ROADSTERS

Collecting and Restoring
Antique, Classic, &
Special Interest Sports Cars

by BOB STUBENRAUCH

Photographs by the author

DODD, MEAD & COMPANY · NEW YORK

The author wishes to express his thanks to Harper & Row, Publishers, Inc. for permission to use material from pages 139–143 in *Horseless Carriage Days* by Hiram Percy Maxim, Copyright 1936, 1937. Thanks also to Alvin J. Arnheim for material quoted from *What Was the McFarlan?* Published privately by Alvin J. Arnheim, 1967, New York, N.Y.

ISBN: 0-396-06799-9
LIBRARY OF CONGRESS CATALOG CARD NUMBER: 73-1652
PRINTED IN THE UNITED STATES OF AMERICA

TO THE MEMORY OF MY PARENTS

ACKNOWLEDGMENTS

I wish to thank the following persons for their generous cooperation:

Jack Foreman, owner and restorer of the 1912 Ford and the Ford Speedster; Norman Viney, owner and restorer of the 1911 Packard; Andrew Adler, owner and restorer of the 1923 Stutz, 1930 Ruxton, and 1937 Cord; Mr. and Mrs. Robert Wells, owners and restorers of the 1926 Lincoln and the 1937 Bugatti; Alex J. Bell, owner and restorer of the 1928 Packard; Robert Carr, owner and restorer of the 1932 Duesenberg; Mrs. Mary Brandman, owner of the 1960 Corvette; Dale Shade, owner and restorer of the 1963 Avanti; Don H. Fellabaum, Jr., owner and restorer of the 1955 Jaguar; James Thomas, owner of the 1957 Thunderbird; and Joseph Hlastan, owner of the 1952 MG.

The 1909 Hupmobile, 1912 Kissel, 1913 Austro-Daimler, and the 1929 Jordan were photographed at the Frederick C. Crawford Auto-Aviation Museum, Western Reserve Historical Society in Cleveland, Ohio. I particularly wish to thank the museum and Kenneth B. Gooding, curator, for his help and the kind assistance of his staff.

The 1914 Mercer, 1929 Mercedes, 1930 Bentley, and the 1932 Marmon were photographed at the Ellenville Motor Museum in Ellenville, New York. I am deeply grateful for the cooperation of Harry Resnick, owner, and Joseph Pettingail, curator.

I would also like to thank William Reynolds, Frank T. Snyder, Jr., and James Gordon. A special thanks is due my wife, without whose patience and encouragement this book could not have been done.

BOB STUBENRAUCH

CONTENTS

FOREWORD

Since the initial explosive tremor of the first internal-combustion engine mounted under a quivering carriage, man has wanted not only to move but to move fast. The early pioneers of motoring, Carl Benz, Hiram Maxim, the Stanley twins, and Henry Ford, rated speed ahead of comfort. Reliability came first, perhaps because it was essential to sustained speed. In the early hectic days of car building, any daring soul with a few thousand dollars could pirate a score of workers from a railroad locomotive shop, rent a barn, and hope for success and automotive immortality. The quickest way to acquire a reputation was to race and beat an established auto. Then as now, racing cars seldom resembled the cars on a dealer's floor, but the very model names conjured up visions of flight. There were raceabouts and runabouts, Speedsters and Sportsters, Flyers and Jackrabbits.

The glory of the names did not mean that all the cars were high-performance types or all in the same league, however. The pseudo sports car, having the appearance and style, but not the abilities, of the performance car, was born long ago: a Model T Torpedo Runabout was hardly a match for a Mercer Raceabout. Purists may shudder, but we will examine the whole field; not only the cars that could do it all—race, handle well, and sustain long hours at high speed to seize the prize—but also those that merely looked as though they could.

The Walter Mitty in every man is realized when he slides into a car that is lower and longer than his neighbor's; when his engine purrs a little louder and a brawny shift lever fits under his caressing hand; when a glittering array of real instruments lets him look into the pulsing engine under the hood then he has a sports car, however capable of competition it may be. As long as cars are made, there will be models designed for those who may never race, but who slide behind the wheel not merely to depart and arrive, but for the sheer pleasure of driving.

BOB STUBENRAUCH

A wide-ranging auto assortment, including models from 1901 to 1953, is represented at a Contemporary Historical Vehicle Association meet in Bluffton, Ohio.

1. EARLY MOTORING

THERE must have been a certain splendor about early motoring, an exhilarating blend of excitement, risk, and challenge. The euphoria, however, was frequently punctured (no pun intended!) by the dirty and strenuous chore of digging out or patching together the often temperamental machines of the day. Until the advent of the Model T, drivers were almost entirely on their own after they left a town's main street. When mired on one of the muddy tracks that passed for roads, the only source of help was the nearest farmer and his yoke of oxen or horses. It was not unknown for an occasional worthy farmer to water a low place in the road, an income producer much like today's "speed traps." Among the early attempts to remedy these churned-up morasses was the corduroy road. This advanced form of road building, probably used by Hannibal to speed his elephants to the Alps, left much to be desired. Eventually the beds of logs laid crosswise would sink out of sight, and the mud would triumph again. Old corduroy roadbeds have been discovered six feet down, when country routes have been rebuilt in modern times.

A mechanical breakdown necessitated locating the nearest blacksmith. Surprisingly enough, they frequently could make serviceable repairs and get the motorist on his way. Against the hazards of bad weather, punctures, bad gasoline, and terrible roads were balanced some genuine pleasures: the lack of traffic, the peace and quiet of driving alone. Finding the way by signpost and milestone was necessary because road maps were still in the future. This led to much asking for directions, and the crafty motorist could dine out in a different home each night by virtue of his distinguished passage in a motorcar.

The decade that gave birth to the auto in America began in 1890, and that period of time also saw the sport of cycling become a national craze. Early motorists frequently compared their trip records to the local bicycle touring club's performance over the same course.

One of those early pioneers was Hiram Percy Maxim. He once said his career in auto making had sprung from a long bike ride home one night after seeing a young lady. The railroads, he mused, had been satisfactory until the bicycle gave people the option of moving when they chose over a route they could personally select. It seemed inevitable to him that they would now want, in addition to these benefits, more speed and less exertion in making their private journeys.

One day in 1899, after a number of auto design successes over several years, young Maxim was motoring from Hartford to Branford, Connecticut, hoping to participate in the first auto race scheduled in those parts. The forty-two mile trip was hampered by deep sandy roads and a bridge out, but he pressed on to finally reach the race-course site. As he told it himself:

As we drove in, seeking a suitable place to pull up and be out of the way of the racers, I noticed with interest that the occupants of the grandstand were waving programs and handkerchiefs. There was no race on and I wondered what the enthusiasm was about. There appeared to be a little Stanley steamer at the starting-line and some kind of low, long thing off at the side of the track with a man underneath it, evidently working on a repair. It afterward turned out that this low, long thing was a single-cylinder Winton gasoline-carriage, the first I had seen.

Then a man came running up to us, full of excitement. He asked me if I were Hiram Percy Maxim of Hartford. I told him in considerable surprise that I was, whereupon he appeared to be extremely relieved. He urged me to hurry right up to the starting-line, explaining that they could have a race! With a sickening feeling I then realized that all the excitement and waving of handkerchiefs in the grandstand was directed at me. It seemed that only three motor-carriages had turned up, the Stanley steamer, the Winton, and my Columbia. The Winton engine could not be started, so that until I arrived there was no chance of a race.

I replied to the urgent pleadings that I had just arrived from Hartford, that I had been delayed on the road, that my machine would have to be fixed up before I could think of starting in a race; but the excited man brushed all my arguments aside by shouting that the crowd had been waiting for hours—that they could not be held any longer—that I must come up to the starting-line at once.

I was swept off my feet. It certainly was a critical situation. I had been through a grueling day, my machine certainly ought to be looked over and tuned up—visions of Lieutenant Eames floated across my mind—"the Pope Company must always win." What in the world should I do!

There seemed no escape. I must go through with the race. Telling the excited one that I would be ready in a moment, I asked Fred Law to unload out of the car everything which could be unloaded, so as to save weight, while I got out the oil-can and squirted everything in sight liberally. By the time I had been over everything, Law had the carriage unloaded and all was ready. With a low spirit, dreading what might be in store for me, regretting I had ever started on such a crazy undertaking, I grasped the crank and started the engine. Hopping into the driver's seat, I ran the little Mark VIII up to the starting-line amid the wildest applause from the grandstand.

When the man in the little Stanley steamer saw that he had a competitor, he hopped out of his machine and busied himself feverishly about it. Then the starter explained to us that the race was to be for five miles, or ten times around the track. By the time the starter had finished his speech I noticed that the Stanley steamer was fairly quivering. It was hissing angrily and seemed ready to burst with the accumulated steam pressure. It was as plain as could be that the Stanley steamer man's tactics were to accumulate the maximum possible steam pressure and then burst ahead and leave me hopelessly in the ruck, hoping that when his steam ran down he would be too far ahead for me to catch him. I realized this was good strategy on his part, but I believed that his accumulated pressure would dwindle away quickly and that when he got down to only what steam he could generate he would not be as fast as I was.

As the starter made ready to give us the starting-signal I speeded up my engine until Mark VIII also was quivering violently. The Stanley had come up to the starting-line first and he had been smart enough to take the pole—or the berth nearest the fence. The pistol-shot rang out above the awful racket and we were off! I let in my clutch on the low gear and Mark VIII made a rush ahead; I snapped into the second as quickly as I dared, and then into high. While this was going on the Stanley man opened his throttle and the terrific steam pressure he had accumulated caused the little steamer to shoot ahead like a dart. By the time I was in my high gear the Stanley was halfway round the track. This looked discouraging, but it did not bother me, because my gasoline-carriage was slowest at the start while my opponent's steamer was fastest at the start. His speed would taper off as he used up his surplus steam pressure, while my speed would hang on and be just as high at the end as at the start. I was short of the three-quarter mark when the steamer passed the grandstand. He received loud cheers as he passed. When I came around I was greeted with loud jeers and the suggestion that I "get a horse."

The next time round I had reached the three-quarter mark when the steamer passed the stand. This was what I had hoped for. It showed that my opponent's pressure was not holding up and that I was moving faster than he. The next time round I was well past the three-quarter mark when he passed the stand. When I reached the stand this time I was the one who received the cheers. The public always sympathizes with the underdog.

It now was all a question of whether old Mark VIII would hold together for five miles. If it did I ought to win. My job was to make it as easy for the little carriage as I could. At the turns I was extremely careful to avoid any undue strains, taking the curves as easily as possible. On the straightaways I hugged the pole closely. Not only was this helpful at the turns, but the road was harder and faster near the pole. Each time round I was closer to the steamer and the crowd cheered like mad. It was a real race and I was overtaking the steamer like an impending fate. About the third mile I caught him right in front of the grandstand amid the wildest yelling and cheering.

Then came the important job of getting the pole. I had to clear him by a generous margin in order to pass in front. At the end of the back-stretch I had enough lead and I closed in and took the pole. The next time I passed the grandstand I had the lead and the pole. Little Mark VIII was plowing along steadily and everything was all right if only she could hold together until the finish. I was more than careful on the turns, and as we neared the end of the five miles I had lengthened my lead considerably. As I swept over the line at the finish I was an eighth of a mile ahead.

The crowd cheered us to the echo, for it had been a real race, after all. I turned and drove back to the finish-line, where my vanquished opponent came forward, shook hands cordially, and congratulated me. It was all over—I had not only reached the race, but had won it. ... And so passed into history the first motor track race in America.

This adventure of Hiram Maxim's was the sort of experience known to just a handful of early pioneers, but many motorists of the teens and twenties would thrill to driving conditions that we view as routine today.

From the brittle pages of a 1917 issue of *The Theatre*, preserved in the collection of Frank T. Snyder, Jr., these zestful lines tell of one driver's joy in jousting with a blizzard in his mighty McFarlan. It was written as a fan letter to the dealer, and that gentleman was astute enough to reprint it in an ad as follows:

S. J. Fleet, Esq.
McFarlan Six Sales Co.
1698 Broadway
New York, N.Y.

My dear Mr. Fleet:

Last Saturday night Mrs. Faversham and I left the theatre at 11:30 to motor down to our place at Lloyd's Neck. We did some tall plowing through virgin drifts of snow, I tell you! It was a sight but the car behaved beautifully. On her high speed she threw up such a tremendous lot of snow it didn't seem to be safe, so we slowed her down to low speed, and then she went through in the most extraordinary manner you ever saw. With the exception of the drifts of snow which she threw to one side, we might as well have been on a smooth road. We really enjoyed the adventure. There was a house party where we were Sunday night. Two of the party motored down in the daytime and had taken different roads to ours to avoid all the snow. They did it in about three hours to three and a quarter. They didn't expect I would come in the car—they thought I would come on the train, and in the morning when they saw my car in the garage, they were rather surprised. At dinner, on my plate, was a boutonniere, with the following poem:

> Oh, Favvy, you're a sweet one.
> And you always were a darlin'.
> But I love you more than ever
> Now I've rode in your McFarlan.

Believe me,

Sincerely yours,
[Signed] William Faversham

The car that coped with those snowdrifts so handily was truly a prestige machine. Produced in Connersville, Indiana, in very limited numbers, the McFarlan was huge, expensive, and built like a Rolls.

It is possible to recreate to some extent today the pleasures of driving as it once was, a somewhat lonely and private experience, the only noise the hum of your engine and the whisper of your Goodyears on dirt, gravel, or blacktop. It is called "shun-piking," and avoiding turnpikes is basic to its success. Pursued one way, it requires careful planning and good maps. Pursued another way, it involves plunging into the back country, selecting roads at random, unaware of what may be over the next hill, so that the pleasures of driving and exploration are intertwined, as they were in those early days of motoring.

2. FINDING THAT VINTAGE CAR

THE person who hunts for an interesting old car has to keep several things in mind simultaneously, even if his search is for a car within a certain age bracket and with specific characteristics. Unless the prospective buyer has ample funds at his disposal, he would do well to investigate all leads that come along, even if the vehicle in question is not just what he is seeking. It is astonishing how often investigating one old car find leads to another. The buyer should acquire the broadest possible general knowledge of old cars even if he is primarily interested in just one make or one automotive era. The opportunity to trade up to the car he wants can be greatly expedited if he is able to recognize an old car bargain of another make or period.

The old car detective should also keep in mind his own limitations of skills or finances when considering a particular purchase. Perhaps it is a very desirable model, an early boattail Auburn or a Leland Lincoln with a custom body; too often, however, enthusiasm for a certain car leads to a rash purchase of a near basket case, far beyond the finances or skills of the buyer. Some basic knowledge of what is involved in restoring the wood, for example, in a classic car could avert an unhappy experience. It has also come as a shock to more than one hobbyist that replacing the leather interior of a Cord or Packard phaeton is not a $200 or $300 job but currently a $2000 or $3000 investment. This is not to say that the old car hobby is solely for the affluent. While the finest restored classics rapidly are becoming out of the average man's reach, many areas of the hobby are no more expensive to engage in than boating, hunting, or stamp collecting.

Where to begin: With these general cautions to keep in mind before deciding on a purchase, just where does one do his shopping for the car he wants? In the early thirties, when the hobby began, every car bug had to beat the bushes himself. Luckily, it didn't take much expertise to find brass-age chariots then. The barns of New England and carriage houses of the wealthy housed antiques and classics by the hundreds. Unfortunately for the hobby, many were brought to light only on their last trip—at the end of a tow rope to the scrap-drive collections of World War II. These days of delightful discoveries and inexpensive

This 1938 Buick Limited was discovered in an Indiana storage garage. It proved to be a rare Model 91 Formal Sedan, of which only 437 were made that year. A good example of a $150 find that could be traded up to a sporty open Buick.

acquisition continued briefly into the postwar period. They are over now, alas, and to make the original discovery of a car thirty to sixty years old requires the skill of Sherlock Holmes and the persistence of Hercule Poirot.

A personal search is still the most exciting and challenging way to uncover and acquire an old car, but fortunately for the novice, it is not the only method. The hobby has grown so in recent years that there are now scores of clubs and many national publications devoted to vintage cars. A detailed list of these organizations and periodicals is included at the end of this book. Thanks to the interest of several hundred thousand auto buffs, one may now sit in the comfort of his living room and consider thousands of cars offered for sale in the pages of club bulletins and other journals. Even more valuable are the ads for scarce and elusive parts, tires, shop manuals, and other vital items needed to complete a restoration project.

Which of the two routes: The principal difference between beating one's own path to that car in a weathered old barn and buying an auto offered by another amateur (or professional) car buff will be this: the car discovered will be a completely unknown quantity, whereas the auto offered in the hobby press may well be partially or totally restored. If it has not been worked on, it will at least have been critically examined and its condition will be known to some degree.

What to pay: The second important difference may well be price. Usually the undiscovered car has remained in its cocoon because the owner has no interest in it. Few people are unsophisticated enough today to give away old cars, as they once did back in the days of opera singer James Melton, but the yardstick of value judgment is likely to rule in the hobbyist's favor with the non-hobby sale of a long-neglected automotive hulk. It may surprise you to learn the wide range of prices that may be asked for old cars by people who are unfamiliar with the realistic prevailing prices. Several years ago I heard

This Marmon was mistakenly advertised as a 1933. It proved to be an earlier "Little 8" model of lesser interest than the legendary V-16s, made through 1933. Vandals had wrecked what had originally been a fine auto.

of a 1930 Model A roadster being sold for $350. To a Ford buff this would appear a bargain. The car in question happened to be brand new, never driven, stored since the day of purchase because of a death in the family. But this once-in-a-lifetime opportunity should be measured against the case of a lady who is still holding out for $5000 for her scruffy Model A Tudor sedan, not worth one-fifth of that sum. Once you have an idea of the prevailing price range you will be in a better position to negotiate the car's purchase. Price determination for antiques and classics is easier than for postwar special-interest autos. Many of the latter cars have been collected for such a short time that no meaningful averages exist.

If a real impasse develops over pricing a car the hobbyist wants badly, he might consider getting the owner to sign an "option to buy" and then later show him hobby ads to establish a fair market value. This writer located a prewar Packard convertible coupe for sale several years ago. The owner was convinced it was a Super Eight and priced it very high, on the assumption it was a full classic. It was a Model 120 and worth much less. I pursued the matter by submitting several recent ads for the correct model, including one with a photo as proof of the model identity. The owner then agreed that my offer was within the prevailing range, and I was able to acquire the car at a reasonable figure.

When you are shopping for a car, membership in a local car club becomes invaluable; most clubs list members who have specialized in certain years and models of a particular make. A phone call may get the precise advice you need. I recently decided to pass up a rather attractive 1933 V-12 Lincoln after an expert restorer of that model advised me of the high cost of the badly needed complete engine rebuild.

If you examine the rise in prices of great cars, you may have mixed emotions.

Spotted at a suburban car wash in 1969, this 1941 Cadillac convertible coupe was for sale at $1500. The car had excellent original green leather interior and a perfect body, marred only by nonoriginal wire wheels.

The front rank of a Long Island used-car lot provided this surprise in 1970. The scarce 1958 Packard Hawk was in fine condition except for noisy bearings in supercharger. This low-mileage car was priced at $950.

If you are selling a car acquired twenty years ago, the tenfold increase in value must be very comforting. Today, the great classics are steadily finding their way into museums and the private collections of wealthy individuals. In 1937, a 1931 Auburn roadster sold for $75, a 1929 Buick Sport coupe for $50, and a 1930 Pierce Arrow coupe for $95. In 1941, a V-16 Marmon listed for $300 and a 1932 Duesenberg speedster for $275. In the middle fifties a 1937 Cord phaeton brought $1250 and a 1936 Ford convertible sedan $95. As recently as the early sixties a custom-bodied Hispano-Suiza brought just $1500 and a 1931 Pierce Arrow convertible coupe $1100, both cars in outstanding original condition. Only three years ago this writer had the opportunity to acquire an excellent 1931 Chrysler Imperial sedan for $1000 and a 1926 Minerva opera coupe for $1250.

Diligent hunting can still turn up buys like these, and there is another consolation for the collector who regrets missing out on the bargain-basement classics of yesterday; the next two decades will undoubtedly see a similar rapid climb in prices for certain postwar special-interest autos. The car buff who does his homework (and legwork!) now may acquire some very scarce autos at very reasonable prices.

The Direct Search: A successful search for an undiscovered "original" old car can be carried out just about anywhere. Techniques will vary depending on whether your local scene is urban or rural.

Wrecking yards have rapid turnover these days except for those located out in the country. A Midwest owner would not "part out" this classic 1941 Lincoln Continental coupe. Asking price in 1969 was $450, as is.

If you are located in a city or its suburbs, you might concentrate on those neighborhoods that were built by the well-to-do in the period between 1915 and 1930. Many of these homes had two or three-car garages, and that factor always heightens the chance that an old car has been kept by the family. A visit to a long-established service station in this area might be productive. Talk to the senior man there or find out if a retired owner or mechanic still lives nearby. Have a calling card or a return-addressed postal card to leave with anyone who seems cooperative. Try not to be too specific in your "wanted-car" description; otherwise you may miss a good lead on a make you haven't mentioned. Paying a fee for a tip that actually leads to a purchase is an accepted practice. Fees mentioned in hobby ads run the gamut from $25 to $100 or more for a really hard-to-find model.

Another possibility is to approach charitable organizations in the area with your request for help. During charity drives these people frequently remove old furniture and clean out garages. You might obtain leads in return for a contribution, should a purchase result. Telephone and appliance repairmen and real estate agents also may know where old cars are hiding. It is important to use discretion and assure any volunteer aide that you will not harass or badger the owner of a car that you'd like to buy.

Negotiations for purchase of an old car may be long and complex or may be finished in twenty minutes. One hobbyist in Ohio admitted it had taken yearly reminders of a tactful nature before a farmer finally sold him a 1909 Model T—fourteen yearly reminders!

While the used-car lots seldom turn up antiques or classics anymore, they are a rich source for postwar special-interest cars. For this you should try the lots in the poorest part of town. Most cars of this type will turn up as "cheapies" or "transportation specials." When the leading new-car dealer gets an unusual twenty-five-year-old trade-in in mint condition, it will usually appear in his showroom with an unrealistically high price on it. Dealers are seldom aware of which models are collectible, and contradictions will appear. A local foreign-car dealer recently sold a 1963 Thunderbird sports roadster, complete with fiberglass tonneau and wire wheels, in mint condition for $750, a bargain for a limited-production special-interest T'bird. Another dealer acquired a standard

An extraordinary find by a fortunate collector. This well-preserved 1932 series-902 Standard Eight Packard will eventually be housed in the car barn under construction in background.

1955 Cadillac four-door sedan in superb condition. On the faulty premise that any seventeen-year-old Caddy must be a classic, this car was tagged at $1995 firm, exorbitant by any scale.

Special-interest cars will be dealt with in a separate chapter, but the techniques are much the same for finding cars of all periods. While combing newspaper classified auto ads, don't neglect the columns listing rummage, garage, or bazaar sales, popular in many parts of the country. In three years of occasional visits to garage sales in small towns in the Midwest, I have seen the following cars: a 1927 Chrysler, a 1928 La Salle, a 1927 Willys-Knight, a 1950 Chrysler Town & Country, several Studebaker Hawks, and a few Packards, including a mint 1946 limo. All were priced below the prevailing hobby market, and none had been advertised in the auto classifieds.

In the direct search method you can cast your net as far as you think practical. The distance you would want to trailer home a non-running find is the usual limit. It is possible that business or a vacation may take you into new territory that appears to provide a mother lode of old cars. The same steps to spread the word can be followed here, but remember that you may have to have your acquisition shipped to your home by commercial carrier. A few firms that specialize in transporting collected cars advertise in the hobby publications.

If the ivy-covered garages behind the English Tudor homes of the twenties are typical of city and suburban vintage car hideouts, barns are the favored

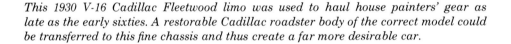

This 1930 V-16 Cadillac Fleetwood limo was used to haul house painters' gear as late as the early sixties. A restorable Cadillac roadster body of the correct model could be transferred to this fine chassis and thus create a far more desirable car.

Shopping for Studebaker parts turned up this first of the Raymond Loewy coupes of 1953. Despite much rust, the car was restorable.

sites out in the country. Here the agents you might want to recruit are well diggers, RFD mailmen, roofers, tractor salesmen, and just about anyone in the small towns who gets out regularly to the nearby farms.

Finds Through the Hobby: In recent years this has been the more usual route in acquiring a car. Prominent among the national journals that serve every aspect of the old car hobby are *Hemmings Motor News, Cars & Parts, Car Classics, Old Cars,* and *Special Interest Autos.* Outstanding among the magazines published by major car clubs are *The Classic Car* (Classic Car Club of America), *Bulb Horn* (The Veteran Motor Car Club of America), and *Antique Automobile* (The Antique Automobile Club of America). This is by no means a complete listing, as new publications continue to appear and new clubs are chartered. The trend appears to be toward more one-make clubs, as the logical answer to the increasingly difficult parts-supply problems. Scarce items such as trim, rubber moldings, and taillight lenses can be put in limited production only when an assured market exists, and the one-make clubs help determine that market.

No discussion of hobby publications can omit mention of what must be the

Rolls-Royce of automotive periodicals, *Automobile Quarterly,* a hardcover magazine-book of outstanding authority and quality.

These publications and the regular bulletins issued by the clubs can provide enormous help in locating the car you want, but there are other sources, such as nationally advertised antique car auctions. Hundreds of cars are sold at prominent auction houses and established old-car museums. Catalogues of autos to be put on the block are usually available long in advance and provision is sometimes made for bidding by mail.

The number of retail showrooms marketing old autos has grown to several dozen across the country. These dealers, who advertise heavily in the major hobby publications, offer cars in every category from antique through special-interest. Most of the dealers prefer to stock mint originals or fully restored specimens, so the cars are priced accordingly. They often offer cars that are very scarce and unobtainable elsewhere.

Many years ago the *New York Times* classified listings started to separate collected cars under the heading of "Antique and Classic Autos." Scores of papers across the country now follow this practice, but the *Times* Sunday edition undoubtedly carries the largest listing. The cars listed, incidentally, are not only in New York City but are located all over the country.

Perhaps the most stimulating way to shop in the hobby is to attend car meets and flea markets. Local events that draw fifty cars can be as much fun as the event that draws an annual rush of fanatic car buffs to Hershey, Pennsylvania, every year. Hershey is the mecca for the most dedicated of old-car enthusiasts and has to be seen to be believed. Motel reservations are seldom available less than eighteen months in advance, and the three-day affair draws tens of thousands of people. When a scarce fender, gauge, or brass lamp can't be found anywhere else, "go to Hershey" is the usual suggestion.

What to Buy: The emphasis on the cars discussed in the profiles in this book is on autos with sporting characteristics. Every enthusiast will be drawn to one make or another. Brass-age cars appeal to some, and classics to others. The twenty-four cars presented here are intended to be representative of each major period: antique, classic, and contemporary or special-interest.

There are, of course, many other makes and models that are extremely desirable. Certain autos are very scarce and may not be seen in a decade of attending car meets. Among these are the Cunningham, the Gardner, the Wills St. Claire, the Brewster, and the Peerless. Production of many interesting cars was small. It should not be forgotten that sheer scarcity alone is an important factor in preserving an old car. Few collectors would dare claim the non-sports 1957 Packard station wagon as an engineering or styling classic, yet it is worthy of saving simply because total production was only 157. Among the nonclassic

This 1930 Chrysler phaeton would be a real find. At $1795 original list it was one of the lowest priced dual-cowl phaetons of the classic era.

Though nonclassic, this sporty 1934 Buick was a quality car. Its beautiful lines make it a desirable addition to any collection.

1929 Model A Ford Convertible Cabriolet probably came closest to providing the working man with an inexpensive, sporty, and practical family auto. Oddly enough, ads usually depicted it in swank and exclusive settings, such as this fox hunt.

17

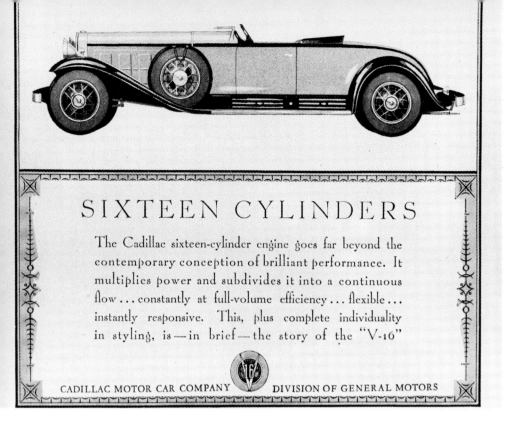

SIXTEEN CYLINDERS

The Cadillac sixteen-cylinder engine goes far beyond the contemporary conception of brilliant performance. It multiplies power and subdivides it into a continuous flow...constantly at full-volume efficiency...flexible... instantly responsive. This, plus complete individuality in styling, is—in brief—the story of the "V-16"

CADILLAC MOTOR CAR COMPANY   DIVISION OF GENERAL MOTORS

One of the few models to rank with the Duesenberg in popularity, the 1930 V-16 Cadillac was a huge, turbine-smooth, 6000-pound road locomotive.

cars of the late twenties and the thirties, certain makes should be considered; the larger-series Buicks, Nashes, and Studebakers included many attractive roadsters, open sedans, and sporty opera coupes. The Studebaker President roadster of 1930 is every bit as typical of that era's "gentleman's sports model" as the classic-status Pierce or Packard roadsters.

Where caution should be exercised is in the amount of time and money that has to be expended on a particular car. This is a touchy question, because it implies that investment is a paramount factor in the old-car hobby. In many cases this is not so. If a 1926 Star or Dodge roadster has a nostalgic appeal to an individual, no one should dissuade him from spending his money to restore that particular car.

It is well, however, to be able to tell a low-grade, common old car with limited collector's appeal, from a desirable, high-quality car. An example of this often-overlooked aspect of old-car collecting was brought to my attention when I visited a restorer's garage workshop recently. A completely dismantled car was undergoing a restoration from the frame up. The cost in time and materials for this effort would be about the same for any similar four-door sedan of the period, assuming the car was purchased in like condition and was complete. The car under restoration was a 1937 Packard 120 sedan. The series 110 six and series 120 eight were the volume, low-priced cars that kept Packard afloat in the mid-thirties. Over 115,000 of these cars were made in that year, and they sold in the $795 to $1250 price range. Had the car selected been a Super

When Studebaker offered the elegant President Eight Roadster in 1929, the company held every official six-and eight-cylinder stock car record for speed and endurance. This luxury model was originally priced at just $1785.

Eight convertible, the restored auto would have been well worth the effort, and as a recognized classic, sure to appreciate in value. While the Super Eight in unrestored condition would have cost more than the 120, the difference would be insignificant in terms of the actual quality of the car, as well as worth.

Some Old Car, Old Barn Adventures: Search out an old car, and you will find yourself caught in the tangled web of someone's old dreams, the waves of nostalgia rolling in as clearly as surf on a Long Island beach. Stand in the doorway of a garage or barn that has not been opened to the light of day for decades, with the owner of the automotive relic that looms in the darkness; prepare to be tactful and properly respectful if you hope to acquire

Any "New Century" series Hupmobile is desirable. The 1929 convertible pictured resembles the LaSalle of the period.

the decayed car you see before you. The original owner sees his Overland or Roosevelt through the rosy glow of his youth. He'll rap a rusty, sagging fender and exclaim, "Good as new!"

Some vintage cars still linger under old tarps in remote barns because the aging owner could no more bring himself to call the junkman for it than toss out his wedding pictures or a tattered family Bible.

After a decade of peering into old barns, tripping over rabbit runs, and getting tangled in old chicken coops, I've run the gamut of people and places in my search for that elusive old great classic motorcar. These owners have been kind and informative, helpful and charming for the most part, but accurate? Never. As a professional photographer I've seen amazing proof that one fuzzy snapshot can lie better than a thousand exaggerating words.

An elderly gentleman offered, by letter, his 1942 Chevrolet coupe. We arranged to meet at his farm, closed since his retirement. His car was described as in "as new" condition. Paint, body, glass—all perfect. The back seat in particular "had never been set in." We met and chatted, and with genuine pride he opened a brass padlock and rolled back the barn door. The weary green Chevy inside the crowded structure almost seemed to squint its headlights in the glare of the sun. Its grille and bumper had long since lost their glitter and had been crudely covered with aluminum paint, the fenders had rusted out heavily at the joints to the body, and heavy globs of lead had been troweled in to fill the larger holes. The door opened easily enough, and a damp cellar smell of mold and mice rolled out of the tattered interior.

The owner beamed with pride as he lifted the hood and exposed the sullen block of rust that reposed under it. He was recounting his travels and adventures in the car while I feverishly struggled to link this ghastly machine with the one described in his letter. There was no conscious deception here, just another owner's inability to separate in his mind the gleaming car he had bought new from the relic it had long since become.

Nor is the older generation alone in their clouded vision. An ad in a small-town paper in the Midwest corn belt caught my eye; a scarce 1934 Nash Ambassador was being sold. A phone conversation with the young owner elicited the information that the car was complete, in good condition, and had always been kept inside. That sounded good, and the reply to my last question about the engine was that it was perfect and "ready for another 50,000 miles."

Barely able to contain myself, I charged off to see this wonder. I was taken to a large barn behind a frame house in town and shown the car. It was hard to determine its make as it had no grille, hood, bumpers, or doors. As my eyes

Locomobile called this massive 1919 factory body style the Gunboat Roadster. Open-style Locomobiles are extremely scarce and much sought.

A custom Imperial Roadster of 1929. Chrysler had Locke design this sleek model, which sold for $2895.

grew accustomed to the gloom I realized the parts were scattered here and there, under a table or leaning against a wall. I peered into the engine compartment. No engine. When I murmured something incoherent to my host, he led me to the building's one small window. "See this?" He was holding a massive crankshaft in his hands. "There's lots of miles left in that. The block is good and a set of gaskets goes with it." Somehow I explained politely that I had expected an assembled car, not a kit. Agreeing with his contention that anyone with a genuine interest in old cars would find it easy fun to restore, I fled the premises.

One provocative ad I answered listed a 1933 Marmon and two old vintage cars of less interest from the twenties, an Essex and a Star. A bell seemed to go off in my mind; a 1933 Marmon could only mean a big car, possibly one of the legendary convertible V16s that car museums prize today. A hasty search in my auto bookshelf revealed that in that last desperate year of Marmon production, only V16s were made, and total production numbered fifty-eight machines! A quick phone call to arrange the rendezvous, and I was on my way. The building in which these cars rested was a carriage house in the old part of town. The adjacent home had been unoccupied for years, and the premises had been vandalized. Holes in the roof had let rain in on the car tops, and the muddy floor was treacherous. I peered into the gloom for the huge body that would indicate the Marmon. All the cars were rusted, glass lay around in shards, and all three cars were quite small. One did have Marmon hubcaps, and a Marmon it was, the "little eight" they brought out in 1928 in an effort to invade the low-price market. Many times old people's memories are faulty, or original titles are missing, or sometimes the car was originally titled incorrectly, all adding up to another disappointing trip.

Sometimes the car you traveled to see turns out to be of no interest, but the visit leads to another machine somewhere else. I went to a Long Island garage some years ago to look at a 1931 Packard roadster. What drew me was the price of $350, low even for that time. The terrible condition of the fenders, holed through and eaten out by rust, cooled my interest. The owner pointed out that fenders could be found, and stressed the fact that the body itself was aluminum. He was right, of course, but the general ruin of the interior and dash convinced me I should have no part of it. (Today such a car would be a buy at ten times the price.) In the same garage the owner had a beautiful original Packard convertible of 1932-33 vintage. The plates still on it, and they indicated it had last been driven in 1938. An elderly widow living nearby had recently sold her home, and the carefully covered Packard had been sold to the first person to express an interest in it. With nothing more than a tune-up and a wax job, this car would have earned 85 to 90 points at any classic car meet.

Every old car buff has his anecdotes to tell, and once hooked, the true hobbyist will follow the faintest of leads, hoping to find that illusory Duesenberg, Mercer, or Stutz awaiting him in some long sealed barn. Even if it is never found, the hunt surely remains half the fun.

A Cadillac offering in the multicylinder race of 1933. The V-12s were fine performers and sold for substantially less than the V-16 line.

The Darrin-designed Packard Custom 180 Victoria of 1941 is a highly prized sports model classic. It originally cost about five times the price of the lowest-price Packard six.

All convertible LaSalles are desirable, although only 1933 and earlier models are rated as classics. This 1934 model is beautifully styled and introduced the pontoon fender line.

Priced at $1495 and $1595 F.O.B. DETROIT

3. THE SPECIAL-INTEREST AUTOMOBILE

IN recent years a new category of car collecting has been created to include cars of distinction that are neither antiques nor classics. The antique definition we refer to is that of the leading old-car clubs and includes the very earliest cars through those made in the midthirties. Certain clubs use narrower definitions of antique, and the cutoff year may be as early as 1915. The "classic car" designation refers to those accredited by the Classic Car Club of America. Both terms are used very loosely in the hobby, it must be admitted, and ads describing a 1960 DeSoto as an "antique" and a 1958 Cadillac as a "classic" were noted recently.

Obviously, many fine cars of superior styling, engineering, or performance are being collected that are not true antiques or classics by definition. The term "special-interest" evolved as a catch-all phrase for cars as different as the American Bantam and the Kaiser Darrin. In terms of vintage, certain special-interest cars of the prewar period are rapidly becoming antiques as well, but will probably retain their original "S-I" status. Other terms have been introduced by some of the newer clubs, such as "milestone" cars, but only time will decide if a standard category will be arrived at and accepted.

This discussion will include cars of both prewar and postwar vintage, with the emphasis on collectible cars of recent years.

The booming interest in these desirable cars stems partly from the sheer scarcity of brass-age antiques and limited-production classics. Other factors are greater availability of parts and easier driving under turnpike conditions. While factory supplies of old parts are dwindling, new clubs spring up and diligently buy dealers' old stocks. The former Studebaker warehouses in South Bend, Indiana, for example, are still in business, and a surprising variety of mechanical, body, and trim parts will be available for many models for some years to come. Brand-new parts are being manufactured for certain cars when the demand is sufficient to make production profitable. The Model T Ford and the popular Model A exist in such large numbers and so many are being zealously restored, that hundreds of replica parts are being produced for these lucky hobbyists.

What are the criteria of a true special-interest car? In the broadest sense, any old auto that someone cares enough about to preserve in fine condition is a special-interest car, at least to the owner. Actually, an "S-I" car should be distinctive in some way. Dramatic styling, unusual engineering, novel construction, limited production are all factors that make a particular car more desirable than the run-of-the-mill production of the period.

Instead of skipping all over the lot, we'll list our selections by make, with comments about certain cars this writer has found fascinating for one reason or another.

Considering our emphasis on cars with sporting appeal, it might be well to mention some fairly recent true sports cars that have survived the test of years and are worthy of being sought out.

The Jaguar and the MG lineage, which are described in detail elsewhere in this book, represent the most popular of the postwar breed of British sports cars.

It may come as a surprise to the younger generation of car buffs, but in England, postwar sports cars were still built with the classic car body techniques of the twenties. That is, hand-formed aluminum sheets shaped over forms to fit onto a substructure of well-seasoned wood. The graceful A.C. coupes and the renowned Morgans were built this way, at a dizzying production rate of five or six a week. In searching out early postwar sports cars it may be noted that they are found in fairly large numbers on the East Coast and in California, mostly because they were originally distributed there.

Among European sports cars of this period, the four-cylinder Alfa-Romeo model 1900 with dual overhead camshafts is one to consider. It may be found in a variety of custom-bodied coupes as well as the factory sedan. Alfas were noted for superb handling, braking, and high speed with good gas mileage.

The list of fine postwar performers includes the Porsche, the Alvis, the Aston-Martin, the Bristol, the Cistalia, the Frazer-Nash, the Lancia, and many others. A surprising number of these cars made between 1947 and the late fifties are currently in the "used-car" price range from $400 to $2500. Most of these will be found in the private sale market; not many are listed in the old car publications. The Sunday *New York Times* sports car columns run to several pages, and these cars turn up in their ads periodically.

The elite motorcars of the sports sets—the Ferrari, the Maserati, and the Mercedes-Benz—require a more substantial investment but offer a wide range of exotic postwar gems. Whether one does his touring in a vintage 1957 Alfa "Spider" at an investment of $800, or drives a gull-wing Mercedes coupe that currently runs to $6000 or more, the postwar era provides the collector with many museum-quality sports cars that are still eminently driveable and even competitive in races or rallies.

One type of auto that came into prominence after World War II may be described as prestige "specials." These designs were based on production-line models and could be produced in limited numbers. The appeal was to customers who wanted something out of the ordinary, a car that would be distinctive and sporty and yet have the familiar feel of their favorite Detroit product. These models were usually top of the line in cost and may have had production runs as low as 500 units. This combination of scarcity and exotic, if not always distinguished, style has made these cars desirable. Rather than to take them as a class, these unusual models will be noted in each make's sketch.

Buick:

This General Motors product seems to be following Packard in acceptance by a growing number of hobbyists who are discovering the fine qualities built into the 1936–1954 Buicks. With the advent of the 120-horsepower valve-in-head straight-eight engine introduced in the 1936 Century model, Buick was on its way with a decade of models that would delight a later generation of collectors. The 1937–38 models are among the most sought after, with the side-mounted convertible coupes and 4-door open sedans considered most desirable. The Century and Roadmaster were hefty cars for these years, weighing from 3832 pounds to almost 5000 pounds for the 140-inch wheelbase Limited series. With relatively high gearing, the 320-cubic-inch "Dynaflash" engine (producing 141 horses in 1938), could move even the massive limo at a steady 70 mph all day long. These very characteristics are among the reasons why the big Buicks are so popular with special-interest fans on today's congested turnpikes.

Desirable models to look for would include, besides all open cars, the opera coupes, the fastback sedans, and the long wheelbase Limited series, some of which had division windows and jump seats.

The interior fittings of these cars were of Cadillac quality, and in fact a very genuine rivalry existed between these two GM divisions. As most Buick buffs well know, body shells were shared by Cadillac, LaSalle, and Buick in these years.

Current prices on prewar Buicks are rising in the hobby, with sound original convertibles ranging from $1500 to $2500. Buying outside the hobby can provide true bargains, though of course, a real effort is required to find the cars. In 1970, a 1941 Roadmaster convertible coupe was noted at $75, another at $30, and a Limited limo at $150. Surprisingly enough, car dealers may often ask lower prices for the infrequent mint trade-ins they get than you would have to pay through the hobby market.

Several Buicks from the postwar period are much sought, especially the 1948 Roadmaster convertible, with its slip-stream-styled fenders, and the original

1953–54 Skylarks. The 1958 Limited is a styling fiasco, but it is scarce and sought in the convertible model.

Cadillac:

Prewar sedans are plentiful, and the price range for the nonclassic models is still moderate. Family resemblance to LaSalles of the same period and, to a lesser extent, to Buicks, is noticeable. The 1938 to 1941 series-60 coupes and sedans might range from $75 to a high of $2000 for one in mint condition. The series-75 models are rated full-classic status by the Classic Car Club of America, and this has undoubtedly enhanced their appeal and value. Surprisingly, the huge limo models, with jump seats and division window, are still reasonable. Although classics, they currently run around $1500 in fair to excellent condition.

Remember that the 1941 and 1942 Caddies were available with Hydra-Matic as well as standard shift. Favorite models are the 1941 convertible coupe and the 1938 to 1941 60-S sunroof sedan. The roofline and window treatment of the 60-Special show a striking resemblance to the 1940 Lincoln Continental.

Prewar Cadillacs with sports characteristics are scarce. Production of the side-mounted roadsters and convertibles was only a fraction of total output, and open cars always find their way to the wrecking yard faster than closed models.

Postwar Cadillacs present several sports models of collectible merit. The convertible of 1947 was noted for the ultimate in pontoon fenders. The first Eldorado of 1953 is sought, as is the lavish brougham of 1957–58. The body design of the brougham differed slightly from the production line model, and the car is readily identified by its brushed stainless steel roof. The two-door fastback models of 1947 and 1948 are attractive, as are virtually all the open Cadillacs right through to 1955. Price range here runs all over the place. A mint 1954 was offered for $75, yet a similar 1952 sedan was tagged at $2000 by a proud owner. Only the limited-production 1957–58 brougham has a well-defined price level, ranging from $2500 to $3000.

Chevrolet:

One is tempted to say that Chevy buffs don't require special models to arouse their enthusiasm. Virtually every model this GM division has ever made may be seen at various meets, usually beautifully restored. The convertibles of any year are collected, but the hot performers started in 1955 with the "power pack" V-8 of 180 horsepower. The 1955–57 models are sought, and the Nomad wagon of the period has a cult of admirers. The Corvette is a Chevrolet, of course, and stands alone in the American sports car category.

The ill-starred Corvair will be saved in large numbers and currently are very low in cost, the attractively restyled 1965 model running about $600.

Chrysler:

Prewar models of the 1938 to 1941 era are not very distinctive in appearance. The really remarkable—and to to this day underappreciated—Chryslers are the extraordinary Airflows of 1934-37. Once you have driven any of these models you will not pass one up. A styling disaster in its time, the Airflow now has a certain charm. It is a difficult car to restore because of parts scarcity, but a sound one in fine condition is a real find. A 1937 Airflow, always chauffeur driven, with less than 50,000 miles, almost mint inside and out, was offered in a small Ohio town recently. The price was finally pegged at $1000 but all the glass needed replacing because the original early safety glass was heavily discolored. Estimates for replacing all thirteen pieces of glass in the car ranged from $400 to $600. Any major problem, such as this mottled glass, should be evaluated before a car is purchased.

Postwar Chryslers offer a variety of interesting models. The long-hood straight eights of 1946 through 1950 were fine road cars. The Town and Country series are much sought, including a coupe and the convertible. With the hemi-engine in 1951 came the short hood and the boxy bodies of the "sculptured look." The best-looking models from 1951 to 1954 are the convertibles and the coupes. The two-door Imperial of 1955 with its free-standing taillights is striking. The 1955 through 1960 "300" performance car series rounds out this list of Chrysler special-interest nominees.

DeSoto:

Prewar models that are prized today center on the Airflow series, which are only slightly different in trim from the Chrysler models. The 1942 DeSoto has hideaway headlights, and of course any prewar convertible should be looked

The 1954 Chrysler Imperial is collectible because only 1200 were made in the two-door hardtop version. With a mint interior and 70,000 miles on the odometer, this easily restored example was rescued from a demolition derby fate for exactly $90.

at, but in general there are few distinctive sports models in this line. Although the make was discontinued in 1961, few postwar models are notable—with the possible exception of the lush 1957 Adventurer two-door hardtop.

Ford:

Whether one calls them antiques, special-interest, or classics, virtually every prewar Ford is collected. In fact, the most desirable models, the 1934, 1935, and 1936 roadsters and phaetons are becoming too valuable to use for everyday transportation. Mint restorations of these models range from $2500 to $5000 and more today. Coupes and sedans, 1935 to 1941, fill the bill nicely for comfortable transportation at reasonable cost. The price range here is currently $300 to $1500.

Postwar models include the wood-trimmed 1946 Sportsman (in great demand), the woody wagons, the 1957 steel-roof "retractable" convertible, and of course, the T'birds. The Thunderbirds are a clan unto themselves, with a sound original 1955 through 1957 two-seater ranging from $1200 to $4000. A possible sleeper is the first of the four-seaters, the 1958 model, which can be found in the $200 to $400 price range. In 1963, Ford turned out a limited run of Thunderbirds which they called the Roadster. Unlike the regular model, the Roadster had a huge fiberglass tonneau with molded race-car headrests and was equipped with wire wheels. Most Fords up to 1951 are of interest, with condition the determining factor in pricing.

What about the Edsel? Is there a future gold mine in collecting a yard full of the forlorn horsecollars? Individuals have done just that. The dream must be turning sour, because a plaintive ad recently offered a dozen Edsels for $1000. A mint specimen for its "used-car" price would make a sensible purchase, but I find it hard to believe that anyone has actually paid $5000 for one, as some sources keep repeating. Over 100,000 Edsels were made in 1958 and 1959. The one that is scarce is the Pontiac-like 1960 model, of which fewer than 2500 were produced. A Toledo, Ohio, used-car lot recently sold one for $95. At that price there is Edsel charisma, but great care should be exercised in evaluating the future value of this rare Ford dud, and none have sports appeal.

The Sports Roadster version of the 1963 Thunderbird was made in low numbers. It featured wire wheels and a novel molded tonneau with slipstream headrests.

This is the Exciting Pacemaker Convertible Brougham

The 1950 Hudson Pacemaker convertible brougham. The rugged six-cylinder engine put out 112 horsepower with a displacement of 232 cubic inches and was a consistent track winner.

Hudson:

Prewar Hudsons were a homely lot. They were well built and frequently introduced novel engineering features, but were seldom beautiful. It is the postwar line of "stepdown" beetle-shaped cars that have earned a loyal following. The number of stock-car races won by these cars is legend. The quality of the ride and the finish of these Hudsons, inside and out, are top drawer. The big six, of only 112 horsepower, gives astonishing performance. Semiautomatic transmission was available in 1950, fully automatic soon after. The most desirable models of the Pacemaker and Commodore series are the club coupe and the convertible brougham. Price range depends on the source of the car. Good buys have been noted this past year from $150 to $400. In the hobby, however, these cars will go much higher. Again, these are cars to be sought and purchased outside the hobby area, if possible.

Kaiser:

All Kaiser-Frazer models are collected, but some exotic models are particularly desirable. One is the Golden Dragon, a 1953 sedan trimmed in an Oriental motif. The roof is covered with simulated woven bamboo in vinyl, and the door handles are gold plated. The 1949 Virginian hardtop and the Frazer four-door convertible are scarce models of limited production. The Kaiser-Darrin sports car with sliding doors in a plastic body is the most unusual of all. The 1954 Kaiser, still a looker, featured a supercharger on the Manhattan model. Kaiser-Frazer prices run from $300 up for a plebeian sedan to $2000 plus for a mint Darrin. This last model, with fewer than 500 produced, should rise rapidly in value.

Lincoln:

Prewar Lincolns that fall in the special-interest area are the Zephyrs. Introduced in 1936, these were the first wind-tunnel-styled cars to win acceptance from the public that had spurned the Airflow. The convertibles are scarce and beautiful. The coupes, particularly the 1938 and 1939, are extremely graceful. All Zephyrs use the much criticized V-12 engine with a modest displacement of 267 cubic inches. They are expensive to rebuild and are considered somewhat underpowered (110–120 horsepower) for the car. Like the prewar Continental the Zephyr is frequently found with another engine installed. Anticipate spending $400 to $1000, if rebuilding the V-12 is required. A 1939–40 Sedan brings $500 to $1500 today, depending on condition. A well-maintained four-door convertible might bring as much as $2500.

Postwar Lincolns through 1948 resemble the Zephyr line, again having the V-12. The big Lincolns with V-8 power and handling that won the Mexican Road Races were made from 1949 to 1951. Open coupes and the Lido closed coupes are the preferred models. The next distinctive Lincoln was produced in 1956–57 when Ford decided to resurrect the Continental designation they had let expire in 1948. Lumping all 1939–1948 V-12 Continentals into a retroactive "Mark I" category, Ford called the sleek, massive new coupe the Mark II. It used many standard Lincoln components, but the body was virtually hand built, as befitted a $10,000-plus car. Most of the 3000 Mark

The Kaiser line offered these limited-run models in 1951, considered much more desirable than the production Kaiser-Frazer sedans.

The 1951 Frazer Convertible America's only 4-door convertible has added convenience, comfort, spaciousness and visibility...of course a fully automatic top!

The 1951 Frazer Manhattan comes in *two* models—one with its metal top coated in glamorous colors, the other with its top covered in shimmering nylon. Either way enhances to the utmost the convertible look in solid steel.

IIs that were made are still running, and the current price range is $2500 to $5000 for a mint specimen. Lincolns made from 1956 through 1960 (other than the Mark II) suffered from extreme styling, the 1958 being 229 inches long. In 1961 Lincoln introduced a new series of Continentals, available only in a sedan and a four-door convertible. Virtually unchanged through 1964, these cars were magnificently made, classic in design, and with quality control not seen in Detroit since Packard built their turbine-smooth V-12 in the midthirties. These four-door convertibles may well be prized classics in 1980 and are being snapped up at "used-car" prices by far-sighted Lincoln buffs.

Mercury:

The original 1939 model is sought in both open and closed models. It differs from the otherwise virtually identical 1940 model in its keg-shaped taillights; the 1940 has flush lenses. There are Mercury "woody" wagons, but the really scarce car built by this Ford division is the Mercury Sportsman. This is similar to the Ford convertible, but only 205 of the wood-trimmed Mercury versions were made in all of 1946.

Packard:

Prewar Packards fall sharply into two groups: the true classics and the bread-and-butter junior cars, the 110 and 120 series. The classic ranked models are the standard and super-8s, and the 12s. Although the 120 series was a cheap car for Packard, it competed with LaSalle, Buick, and the big Stude-

Packard celebrated their fiftieth anniversary in 1949, and the Custom Eight convertible was a popular model. On a 127-inch wheelbase, the car featured power options; the traditional straight eight was rated at 160 horses.

Limited-production 1954 Packard Caribbean featured the last version of the famed straight eight. With nine main bearings, the 212-horsepower engine displaced 359 cubic inches.

bakers—all of which were quality autos. Packard parts are readily available, and the Packard name still carries prestige on the road. However, expensive restoration that might be worthwhile on a classic Super-8 would not pay on a 110 sedan. Good condition should be a prerequisite in considering a bottom-of-the-line prewar Packard. The exception is a scarce model, such as the convertible coupe. Price range for this 1939 120-open car should run from $500 for one in shabby condition to $2600 for one in nearly perfect shape.

Postwar Packards to consider are the attractive Clippers made in 1946–47, the bulbous "bathtub"-styled 1948–50 models, and the series that ended in 1956, the last true Packards. The standout model is definitely the Caribbean, made as a nine-bearing straight eight in 1953–54 and as a V-8 in 1955–56. The Ultramatic transmission and the novel load-leveler of these last years had bugs and may provide problems in service and parts today. A personal favorite is the 1953–54 Caribbean convertible with the traditional straight eight at its most potent development, 212 horsepower. The 1948 Custom Eight convertible is another attractive model in great demand.

The Packard crest was carried on Studebaker-built cars in 1957-58, and these interesting cars are worth saving simply because of their scarcity. Total production of the last Packard station wagon, for example, was a paltry 157 units!

Studebaker:

Prewar Studebakers are well-built quality machines. Styling was clean and attractive, the 1940–42 models having unusually large areas of glass. The Champions were very low-priced cars and had just carved a niche in the $500 auto market when the war ended production.

Last fling for Packard—having its name and hub caps on this face-lifted Studebaker Golden Hawk. With a genuine leather interior and 275-horsepower supercharged engine under the hood, only 546 of this model were built.

The bold new 1948 Studebakers were most attractive in the convertible and Starlite coupe models.

The Raymond Loewy-styled Studebaker introduced a European line to the South Bend car and created a sensation. The coupe was just 56 inches high.

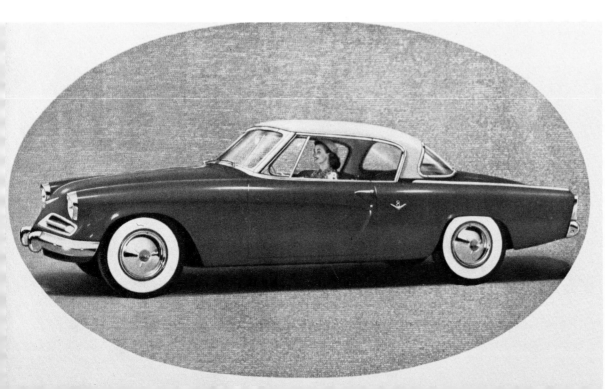

After the war, Studebaker, like Packard and others, had full coffers and could compete strongly with the big three. In one of their wisest decisions, the Studebaker brass called in Raymond Loewy's design team to create their new car. The short hood, flat rear deck, "is it coming or is it going" Studebaker was a winner. A 1947 Starlite coupe with its airplane-like greenhouse, still looks very contemporary twenty-six years later. This coupe and the convertible of 1947–49 are good choices. The 1950 jet-nose is a model that you either love or hate.

Styling just marked time on the 1947 theme until 1953 when Studebaker created their all-time design landmark. The beautiful coupe and hardtop of that year have been rated by car magazines and art museums as the most beautiful car made in America. The so-called Loewy coupe handled well, particularly the six, but all through the later Hawk versions, it suffered from body problems. Doors stuck, windows rattled, and the car would rust away if you left a bag of salted peanuts in the glove compartment overnight.

It is a tribute to the design that so many car buffs are now restoring these sport coupes. Much sheet metal remains in stock in South Bend for postwar Studes, and only the trim presents a problem. Recommended models are the 1955 limited-production Speedster and the 1953–55 Champion or V-8 President hardtop. The price range here is incredible; I junked a restorable 1955 for $7 for lack of storage space a few years ago. The determined shopper can acquire a sound coupe for $100 requiring work, or a mint restored car in the $800 to $1500 range.

There are many other makes and models that fall in the special-interest category. The delightful American Bantam was followed by another attempt at a miniature car in the postwar years, the Crosley. The station wagon version of this car resembles a large refrigerator tipped on its side and equipped with four wheels. Willys, which had produced a series of compacts in prewar days, ended their passenger-car efforts in 1954–55 with the Aero-Eagle, a well-designed compact car about ten years ahead of its time. Nash in 1949 produced a huge streamlined car called the Airflyte. One look at the instrument panel should intrigue any car buff; called the Uniscope, it resembled a space-capsule pod, with all dials in a cluster on the steering column. This car was a further development of the Lincoln Zephyr concept, of form following function in a wind-tunnel-designed body. Today, this scorned "bathtub" Nash is a real sleeper and would probably command all of $75 at a budget used-car lot.

The appeal of these recent postwar automobiles is in having a second chance at predicting which cars will be rated worthy of preservation and in the opportunity of acquiring them at bargain basement prices. You may never find that Duesy in the barn, but finding a mint 1953 Loewy Studebaker coupe in a heated garage with just 11,000 miles on the clock for $200 can be a real thrill too.

A small town meet in the midwest. Model years range from 1913 to 1951. The big, white-roofed sedan at left is a Duesenberg.

4. FLEA MARKETS, MEETS, AND CARAVANS

MOST of us have had the experience of being out for a Sunday spin and suddenly coming upon a sedately paced and glittering convoy of old autos, headed for some unknown and mysterious destination. To the novice the thought arises, just what can one do with a valuable antique or classic car into which years of labor, money, and love have been poured? Briefly, you drive it. The nub of old-car fascination for most dedicated buffs is the rare thrill of reliving motoring as it used to be in a vehicle that you yourself have rescued from oblivion.

Over the years, with the growth of the hobby and the formation of scores of clubs, certain car events have become highly formalized. These can be broken into meets, where cars are judged, and tours and caravans, in which owners assemble to travel together to a common destination. A third type of gathering is the flea market, an informal marketplace where car buffs flock for a day or two, to search out parts needed for their restoration projects.

A brief description of an Ozark caravan might give an idea of others that are held all over the country. The Classic Car Club of America hosts an annual caravan, and a recent one began in St. Louis, Missouri. About a hundred classic cars from twenty-one states gathered at St. Louis and from there proceeded south to Hot Springs, Arkansas. This 500-mile tour was conducted at a leisurely pace to ensure time for side excursions. A successful caravan is planned to cover scenic countryside, interesting historic landmarks, and hopefully, an old-

Part of the fun is the occasional embarrassment of an engine conking out in a Main Street parade.

(Top left) The gamut here runs from MG to Cadillac, with a rare European convertible in center foreground. (Top right) Once a popular accessory of the thirties, flag holders are now a prized touch for parades. (Above left) A final touch-up before the judges arrive. (Above right) The automotive heritage of Auburn, Indiana, is remembered annually when the Auburn, Cord, Duesenberg Club arrives in polish and glory. (Left) Before the Auburn parade this 1937 Cord gets some helping hands and advice from other hobbyists.

car museum or two. This tour included the sights at Petit Jean Mountain in Morrilton, Arkansas, where the superb Winthrop Rockefeller auto collection is housed.

The seasoned hobbyist undertakes this sort of tour with a trunk full of spare parts, knowing he will not find a 1936 Packard Super Eight fuel pump at the average truck stop on Interstate 44. The combined expertise of several score car buffs usually enables necessary repairs to be made, and a caravan is a much more secure way to travel great distances than to tour individually. Radio communications between the leaders and the rear-guard member of such a convoy (which may have over a hundred vehicles) is a factor in the good safety record maintained by the major clubs. The social pleasures of being among other car enthusiasts are of course a great attraction of these tours.

Those same cars, traveling singly or in pairs all in the same general direction, are probably headed for a meet. It might be a prestigious event like the Greenfield Village Old Car Festival, held annually at the Henry Ford Museum in Dearborn, Michigan, or a regional Grand Classic meet, or one of hundreds of smaller events held locally from spring through fall. (In this hobby, winter is work time and the warm months are show time.) While the regional meets of the senior clubs may draw hundreds of cars, local events with a casual gathering of a few dozen cars and their owners can be just as enjoyable. The national hobby publications take pains to publish virtually all meet schedules made available to them.

The rating and evaluation of a restored or original-condition car in such a competition is a complicated procedure governed by rules worked out over many years. The basic premise is that a fine restoration does nothing more or less than recreate the auto as it was when it left the factory. To accomplish this, restorers go to incredible lengths. On one car in which early safety glass had to be replaced, the restorer went to the trouble of reproducing the maker's name on the corner of each window. Plastic material is not used when replacing running board rubber; indeed, matting with an incorrect pattern will cause points to be deducted from the car's point total. Hence the limited production, at relatively high cost, of certain patterned rubber matting for classics such

Parade time in Auburn, Indiana.

The aristocratic Duesenberg, being closely admired.

as Cadillacs and Packards. Although new parts may be reproduced and incorporated into a restoration, an entire replica body is not considered cricket for competition. In a car of great value and scarcity, a dual-cowl V-16 Cadillac phaeton, for example, the most vestigial remnants of a body could be restored and still be considered authentic. Ideally, a restored car is one that is completed with a maximum of original parts and a minimum of newly manufactured parts.

What do judges look for? Completeness is one factor. A convertible should have the correct boot for storing the top, and older touring models should have the side curtains as originally fitted. All equipment—radios, wipers, lights—should work. Sealed-beam headlight inserts in cars before 1940 will usually lose points. Owners of brass-age chariots who like to drive to meets frequently use clip-on supplementary lights that can be quickly removed for car judging.

When one considers the number and variety of grading categories, which in one club dedicated to contemporary cars includes sixteen areas from glass to tires, it seems miraculous that any car can achieve a 100-point, or perfect, score. The passion for perfection has risen to the point that some museums and collectors have taken a car that was fully restored some years back, and starting from the frame up, have restored it even further. Perhaps the last word on how far this can go was heard from an elderly gentleman at a classic meet recently. He expressed the opinion that a particular gem being admired was truly beautiful, but that it had never looked as good when first made! It appeared he had once been a supervisor in the custom body shop that made that very car. This emphasis on perfection has led to the use of the expression "for go or show." Few 100-point cars are regularly driven, and a brief trip could well require minor work in order to retain that magic century point score.

The serious judging, the moment of truth when the restorer puts his handiwork to the critical test of a jury of critical and knowledgeable experts, is not all that transpires at meets, however. Car owners may indulge in various games to show off their command of their cars. One fun event involves a team, consisting of a driver and a partner who endeavor to spear potatoes out of tires laid out along a winding course. This kind of tomfoolery, usually indulged in by the owners of agile Model Ts or Model As, is frowned on by some but very much enjoyed by others. Few American events really test the acceleration or speed of our great classics, but in England, it is routine to punish forty-year-old cars in sprints or rugged hill climbs.

To a really hooked hobbyist, a good flea market can be even more enjoyable than a car meet. One never knows what will turn up, and there is always that lucky find of a scarce accessory for a particular car that gives the final touch to a fine restoration. This may be a running board spotlight, an authentic trunk the owner despaired of ever finding, or a new "old stock" steering wheel for a cracked original that is beyond repair.

Owners as well as part and full-time professional dealers attend these events and set up their lots in intriguing profusion. At the annual event in Hershey, Pennsylvania, an unbelievable total of 2000 stacks of automotive parts, from rusty steel to brassy treasure, has been offered for perusal and purchase. This affair, which has grown up around the regional meet of the Eastern Division of the Antique Automobile Club of America, and is always held for three days in the fall, has become a national attraction. Over 1200 old cars were shown at a recent "Hershey," and scores of cars changed hands. It is not unusual

A valuable assortment of mascots and hub caps spread out for inspection at the Auburn meet.

A gleaming fiberglass Kaiser Darrin parades at the annual meet in Bluff-ton, Ohio.

Why did she quit? Grim concern quickly proved unfounded, as this 1917 Studebaker proved to be suffering only from a clogged carburetor.

Time to add up the scores, as judging is completed at a typical meet.

to see a decrepit Model T tagged at $300 near a sound original Duesenberg offered at $33,000. It is a gargantuan combination of major meet and spectacular flea market. As an educational step in entering the old-car hobby, the Hershey event should not be missed.

Perhaps the most enjoyable kind of touring is the local run, in which people in one club who know one another take a casual impromptu drive over familiar roads. On such a run some years ago I was fortunate enough to ride in a great brass-age Case; my young boys rode in the lofty back seat, thrilled to the core. At dusk our convoy of a dozen cars wound through the back country roads, a Rolls Silver Ghost, a Jackson, a Cadillac, a Sears, and other big and little gems. Our headlights and acetylene gas lamps picked us out on the darkening horizon as a string of jewels. The unfamiliar chugs and snorts brought people to the doors of their farmhouses, and their smiles revealed an instant rapport between viewer and participant. At a railroad crossing on a dirt road the convoy waited patiently as a late commuter train trundled its load of city workers back to suburbia. In its windows a blurred panorama of disbelieving expressions gawked at this apparition of another age. Perhaps these hobbyists are carrying nostalgia for the past to its ultimate expression. Those who do it know it is a unique experience, and worth all the effort.

Huge Dietz gas lamps, pin-striped semielliptic springs, and big wire wheels were typical equipment on many brass-age runabouts. The car is a Series J, type 35 Mercer.

5. THE ANTIQUE ERA

For autos of sporting characteristics, the antique era can be defined only vaguely. At the lower end chronologically, models described by their makers as runabouts, semi-racers, or speedsters were proliferating well before 1910. At the upper end, when certain cars of the twenties began to acquire the qualities of the classic era, some autos would have to be called both antique and classic, such as the later Mercer Raceabouts of the early twenties.

There is one sharp line of demarcation, however. That is the end of the brass age and the beginning of the period during which the layout and shape of the automobile became stabilized. The brass age ended around 1912, and with the introduction of electric lights, the rounded "streamlined" body, and the self-starter, the modern car had arrived. The change between a 1910 model and a 1916 model of almost any make is startling. The first is open and exposed; shift lever and running boards, lights and windshields, all are separate and bright with brass or plated trim. Gas tank, bucket seats, and the very running gear are clearly visible. Over the next five or six years, all this changed. Flowing lines concealed the components of the car, giving it the general shape it would have for twenty years to come.

It is not surprising that we are more fascinated by the fine cars of the brass age than by their immediate successors. The polished wood dashes, the bright colors, the gleaming trim, and the exposed chains or shaft drive are clearly of a different age. More dramatic progress in the development of the motorcar was made from the turn of the century to 1910 than in any other decade since.

1909 HUPMOBILE
TWO-PASSENGER RUNABOUT

TOWARD the end of its first decade, the automotive scene in America was marked by a surge of incredible activity and growth. Ford, for example, had made profits of over a million dollars in 1907, even before the legendary Model T was born. Business at Packard, Olds, and Buick was booming, and over two hundred other companies were striving to perfect cars that would bring the auto-hungry public streaming to their showrooms.

It was a period of free-wheeling experimentation. The days of one and two cylinders were definitely over, save for those few conservative farmers who found the buggylike "high wheelers" comfortably familiar in appearance. Auto makers were tinkering with every conceivable method to make an engine start from the driver's seat; they were beginning to rethink having the wheel on the right side; and those who hadn't standardized on four-cylinder engines were testing six and eight-cylinder designs.

Robert C. Hupp had had positions in this decade of growth that equipped him for the complex task of producing his own car. He had been service manager with Olds and Ford and then moved up to production supervisor at Regal Motor Cars in Detroit. In 1908, he found backers and established the Hupp Motor Car Company in Detroit. As was then common practice, Hupp became president, and the financiers, Joseph and Walter Drake, were vice-presidents, while John E. Blake became secretary-treasurer.

The first machine they offered to the public was the model illustrated, the Model 20 runabout. It was ready in time for the Detroit Automobile Show of 1909 and was an immediate success. Many cars were available in its $750 price range, but few offered as much for the money. The 20-horsepower, four-cylinder L-head type engine was well designed and well built. Its three main bearings were of Parsons white bronze, and the Breeze carburetor had an ingenious device that used warm air directed from the exhaust manifold to minimize stalling at low speeds. The high-tension Bosch magneto was a costly unit never before used as standard equipment on a car in this price range. The transmission was simpler to operate than the planetary set on the newly

(Opposite) The low and Sporty Model 20 weighed only 1100 pounds fully equipped. The gas headlamps were a $25 accessory. (Photography by permission of the Frederick C. Crawford Auto-Aviation Museum, Western Reserve Historical Society, Cleveland, Ohio.)

The first Hupmobile was built on an 86-inch wheelbase, and in true raceabout fashion was designed without doors.

introduced Ford Model T. The lever was moved back for low, forward for high, and to the side for reverse.

Aluminum was used for the steering wheel, and steering was by rack and pinion. This first model sported a cut-out entrance, without doors, and its 86-inch wheelbase and weight of 1100 pounds made it a nimble as well as a jaunty-looking performer. Hundreds of minor and major races were run yearly in those competitive days, and the winners trumpeted the details in their advertising. What made the Hupp impressive in the Brighton Beach contest of August, 1909, was its startling ability to outdistance cars that cost three and four times as much.

Over 1600 Hupmobiles were built and sold this first production year of 1909. In fact, the entire year's production was sold out in six months, and deposits had to be returned to hundreds of would-be buyers. A second plant was hurried to completion for the planned increase of cars for 1910. Advertisements urged the public to "Chat with a Hupmobile Owner" (shades of "Ask the man who owns one")! They flatly claimed that the total operating cost of the sprightly runabout, including oil, gas, and repairs was twenty-five cents a day. This was "cheaper than street cars—infinitely less expensive than a horse."

Other makers, such as Reo and Packard, had run their cars from coast to coast to demonstrate reliability, but in their second year, Hupmobile sent a Model 20 around the world. This 18,000-mile test was completed without difficulty in 1910. The success of the Hupmobile can be fully appreciated by comparing it with a competing make. Buick offered a Model 32 runabout with similar specifications and within $50 of the Model 20, yet the Hupp Company increased production to over 5000 cars in 1910.

In 1910 the Hupp brothers expanded their interests in many directions, like a miniature General Motors. Their subsidiaries included foundries, machine shops, two other car companies (Monarch and Rotary Valve), a construction company, and of course the noted Hupp-Yeats Electric Auto Company. Robert Hupp resigned from the presidency to form the Hupp Corporation, and set up factory branches in half a dozen cities.

The Model 20 was succeeded by the outstanding "32" in 1912. The Swedish reliability run of 1913 drew sixty-eight contenders, and a Model 32 Hupmobile came in first. The reputation of the car grew, although only one model design was made during the war years. Production reached 38,000 by 1923. After a brief experiment with an eight, the company abandoned the reliable four and produced six-cylinder cars in 1926.

Styling was not usually considered the forte of the Hupmobile. Rather, sound engineering, quality construction, and easy handling for the value-conscious buyer were its attractions. In later years, the series E eight-cylinder roadster and the New Century series of 1933 were stylish indeed.

(Left) Lever-operated emergency brake to the rear wheels is mounted adjacent to the gear-shift lever. Transmission provided two speeds forward and one reverse. (Below) The cockpit was austere; long pedal between clutch at left and service brake at right is the accelerator. Note right-hand drive, still popular in 1909.

The company floundered badly in the depression, but economic conditions were responsible for this, not the product, which was always an attractive value. The figures speak for themselves: 65,862 cars built in 1928 compared to 7316 vehicles in 1933.

The Aerodynamic line introduced in 1934 was extremely competitive, and three model lines were available in a total of five body styles. The new styling and richly trimmed cars reversed the sales graph for the first time in years and drew close to 10,000 buyers. In 1935 the slide, only momentarily arrested, began again. The company slashed its basic model to an all-time low price of $695, but sales continued to decline. While the management team struggled through a wilderness of problems, a stockholders' suit succeeded in replacing the board of directors, and in 1938 a new effort was made to stay afloat with a conventionally styled car. The business recession, which hurt all car makers, virtually doomed this model, and only 1700 cars were made.

One last gamble was taken by marketing a face-lifted 1937 Cord sedan with a Hupp six-cylinder engine. Government loans and a deal with Graham Paige almost brought this off. Orders poured in from buyers who had 1940 war-production paychecks in their pockets and were anxious to have an "almost" Gordon Buehrig Cord for one third the price of that earlier style leader.

The final irony was that Hupmobile, always known for building a solid car, couldn't put these ersatz Hupp Skylarks together. The Cord dies were made for a limited run and could not be adapted to volume production in time.

The 1909 runabout pictured is one of the earliest Hupmobiles existing, bearing Serial Number 52. It was purchased for the Frederick C. Crawford collection in 1940 and was restored in the noted Cleveland Auto-Aviation Museum shop. Mr. Crawford delighted in driving the car, and the restored vehicle completed the Glidden Tour in 1946.

Although Ford is generally credited with putting "America on wheels" with the Model T, it should be remembered that other fine cars were being built at the same time. The original slogan of the Hupmobile was rather pompous, and few remember it today: "A Car of Napoleonic Proportion." Perhaps the slogan they used in those last rocky years is a better epitaph: "Hupp—Always Built A Good Car."

The rugged four-cylinder, water-cooled, L-head-type engine with 3¼ bore and 3⅜ stroke. The simple design featured cast-in-pairs cylinders and three main bearings, and was equipped with the Bosch magneto.

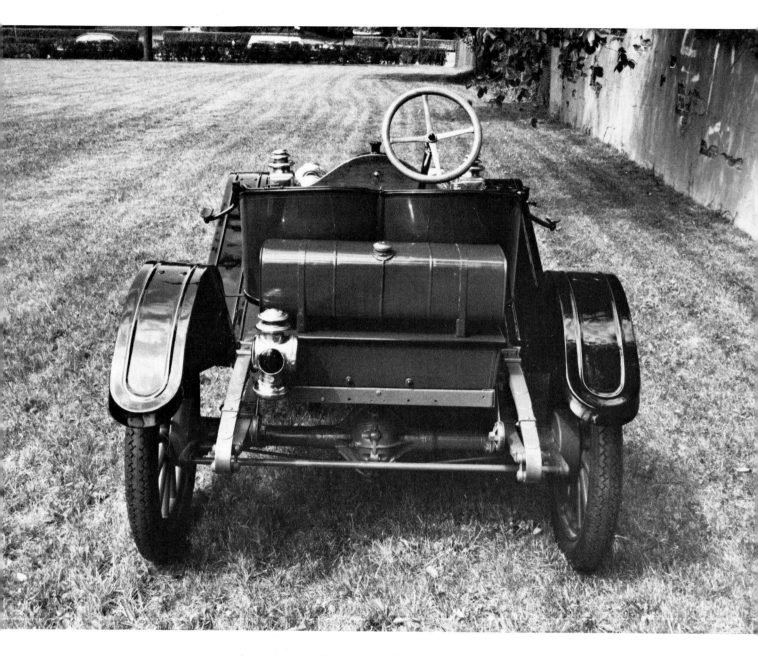

Rear view of the Model 20, showing the large elliptic springs.

Full dash instrumentation consisted of a Warner speedometer and odometer.

Timing the engine was facilitated by numbers that the factory engraved on the huge flywheel.

Still selling for $750, the popular runabout sported doors and mechanical improvements in 1912.

Runabout
Fully Equipped

Hupmobile
GUARANTEED FOR LIFE

$750
F.O.B. Detroit

For 1912—Complete Equipment Included

Note the inclined gas tank and external gear-shift lever of this Kissel Semi-Racer. (Photography by permission of the Frederick C. Crawford Auto-Aviation Museum, Western Reserve Historical Society, Cleveland, Ohio.)

1912 KISSEL KAR
SEMI-RACER MODEL 4-40

ONE OF THE stalwarts of the German-American community in Hartford, Wisconsin, around the turn of the century was Louis Kissel. This energetic immigrant had progressed from farming to manufacturing agricultural equipment and stationary gas engines. His efforts prospered, and with the aid of his four talented sons he rapidly branched out into other areas. They soon owned an electric company, and the Hartford Plow Company, and in 1906 became housing developers. With typical thoroughness, they acquired the stone quarry, lumber mill, and sand pits necessary for mass construction of homes. This penchant for controlling all stages of their products was to be repeated when they launched the Kissel auto.

After announcing the family goal of producing a new, quality car, two of the sons, George and William, began construction of a four-cylinder engine in the shop of their plow factory. The 18-horsepower design was a success, and after a hand-built prototype proved its mettle, the family entered the auto field in June of 1906 as the Kissel Motor Car Company. They decided to begin with an assembled car until skilled workers could be found to produce a distinctive Kissel-designed machine. The reliable 35-horsepower Beaver engine, the Timken axle, and Warner gear box were used, and almost one hundred cars were produced by 1907.

The arrival in 1906 of Herman Palmer was to solve the engineering needs of the fledgling company. This unassuming man had taken a general shop position and almost accidentally revealed that he had trained in engineering at the University of Cologne. He prepared the groundwork for the 60-horsepower big six, which established the Kissel Kar as a really powerful machine. In 1908 another new arrival, J. Frederick Werner, was soon to provide the company with auto bodies of comparable quality. Werner, who had come from the Opel plant, was a graduate of the long, arduous apprentice system of imperial Germany, and was now a master coach-builder. His father had actually handcrafted coaches for King Ludwig II of Bavaria.

Several outside firms provided Kissel bodies until 1909, when by good planning both the new 60-horsepower engine and the factory body were ready for produc-

Deeply crowned fenders graced the low-slung Kissel. The rugged front axle is drop forged.

Twin spares were carried on slanted rear deck of the 4-40 Kissel.

(Left) Right-hand drive with shift lever and emergency brakes mounted outboard. (In 1914 Kissel moved the wheel to the left and drive controls to the center of the cockpit.) Acetylene tank provides gas for the big Vesta headlights. (Above) Instrumentation on dash consists of clock, Bosch ignition, and a speedometer calibrated to 75 mph. The three pedals, from left to right, are clutch, accelerator, and service brake.

tion. The Kissel Kar was now moving into a full range of models, including the 6-60 touring car on a 142-inch wheelbase. A semi-racer model of this series won the 1910 Los Angeles to Phoenix race, impressively clipping three hours from the previous record.

Kissel combined staid Germanic quality with surprising innovations, including the first version of what would be called today a wraparound windshield. Their engineers were hot on the heels of Cadillac with a practical electric self-starter, and electric road lights were offered in 1912. Touring was now coming of age; free highway maps were being given out at Gulf gas stations, and in Cleveland, electric traffic lights had replaced the traditional hand-operated semaphores.

Kissel was now an accepted make, relying on their refined big-six engine and the overall quality of their machine. They were brave enough to try to outdo Packard, when that maker's brilliant new twin six was drawing crowds to every Packard showroom. They introduced the huge Kissel Double Six, which used the untried Weidely V-12 as a power plant. This cranky engine was no Packard and was dropped after fewer than a thousand cars were built and before it could besmirch the Kissel name.

(Opposite, top) The right side of the 4-40 power plant. Cylinders cast in pairs allowed Kissel to offer a two-pair "four" and a three-pair "six". (Opposite, bottom) Left side of the 4-40 engine. Note the fan guard ring.

(Above) The inclined gas tank and slanted tire rack improve the lines of the Semi-Racer. (Right) Solid Kissel workmanship is evident in the hefty steering wheel.

Brass step plate carries the maker's name.

(Left) Horn and sidelamp of the Kissel. (Below) Rear detail shows semielliptic springs, huge rear brake drum, and standard taillamp.

From a collector's point of view, the great landmark cars in the quarter century that Kissel made autos should include the first several models, those from middle periods and the last year's models. The Semi-Racers of the prewar years were the equal of many cars of more lustrous marques. The famed Silver Special Speedsters and the legendary Gold Bug of 1918–19 were to Kissel what the Playboy was to be to Jordan. They fired the public's romantic imagination as no previous Kissel-built car had.

The final product of the Hartford factory was the logical development of the Gold Bug. In 1928 the big six gave way to a straight eight of 115 horsepower, and the White Eagle Speedster was offered. The ads proclaimed it "The king of straight eights—a Niagara of power—100 miles an hour for red-blooded Americans who demand speed at its speediest." While this most beautiful and sporting Kissel was made for just two years, some 1500 were produced, and today it is probably the most desired model of the make.

Like so many others, the Kissel Company died sooner than the quality of its product merited. A complicated merger with Moon, Gardner, and Ruxton, under the name of New Era Motors, fell apart in the fall of 1930. Kissel asked for receivership and was declared bankrupt in February of 1931. In the crash of 1929 and the depression that followed, there were simply too many fine car makers for the dwindling market to support.

The Kissel Kar shown in the photo profile was offered in 1912 as a lighter version of the record-breaking big six. This model 4-40 is powered by an L-type four-cylinder engine developing 40 horsepower. It features a Stromberg carburetor, a circulating oiling system, and Bosch dual ignition. The transmission is a three-speed gear set. A full floating rear axle and rear wheel brakes with both internal and external shoes were unusual advances for the day.

S. Sipple of Lorain, Ohio, restored this bright red machine; it was a "frame-up" project. New fenders were duplicated from the originals, exact replicas were made for the foot pedals, and a new gas tank was constructed.

While the company flourished, Kissel represented the solid virtues of German mechanical skill and American innovation. At the end they added those rare ingredients that turn dry records into legends. They built motorcars of solid dependability coupled with classic grace and style. In the words of one of their last ads: "White Eagle—emblematic of daring, courage, speed, power! . . . As only Kissel could build it."

A few models of the Kissel line for 1925.

KISSEL

De Luxe Phaeton
Sixteen hundred eighty-five dollars

Speedster

Brougham-Sedan

Packard runabout is so well proportioned it appears considerably longer than its actual wheelbase of 108 inches.

1911 PACKARD MODEL 18 GENTLEMAN'S SPEEDSTER

AN EXPLOSIVE display of temper by the Cleveland car builder Alexander Winton is supposed to have caused the Packard brothers to make their first automobile. Every historian finds a different version of this legend, depending on whose memoirs he reads.

The facts are that James Ward Packard and William Dowd Packard had long considered entering the automobile field. The dispute with the hot-tempered Scotsman, which occurred in 1898, arose from what James Packard thought were major shortcomings in his new Winton, the twelfth one out of the factory. Five years earlier, during a European visit, he had driven and purchased a De Dion-Bouton tricycle, one of the most reliable gasoline-powered vehicles of the day. The Packard brothers were successful manufacturers of electrical products, and very likely James bought the Winton for the same reason he had brought his French tricycle home to Ohio; namely, to see what made it tick.

He must have thought that the Winton product had some merit because he promptly hired away the shop superintendent J.W. Hatcher, and one of the founders of the company, George Weiss. The Packard brothers incorporated under the name of the Ohio Automobile Company, setting up shop in Warren, Ohio, in 1900. From this point on, James became more involved and his brother William less interested, finally devoting all of his time to their electrical-products concern.

At the time of incorporation, the first Packard built had been running almost a year. Little more than a self-propelled buggy, it was remarkable in having a top speed of 35 miles per hour, smoothly reached by means of a three-speed gearbox. Its one-cylinder engine delivered 12 horsepower and featured an automatic spark advance invented by James Packard. This single-seater was steered by tiller and was chain driven. Much impressed by the success of the curved-dash Olds, Packard believed the future lay in concentrating on one-cylinder machines. He went so far as to write a booklet on the fallacy of multicylinder cars entitled *Six to One, or Wasted Pride, Perspiration and Profanity*. Strange words, indeed, from the man whose twin six would amaze the public fourteen years later.

(Opposite) The distinctive radiator shape Packard was to carry for a half century was already well defined in the 1911 model 18.

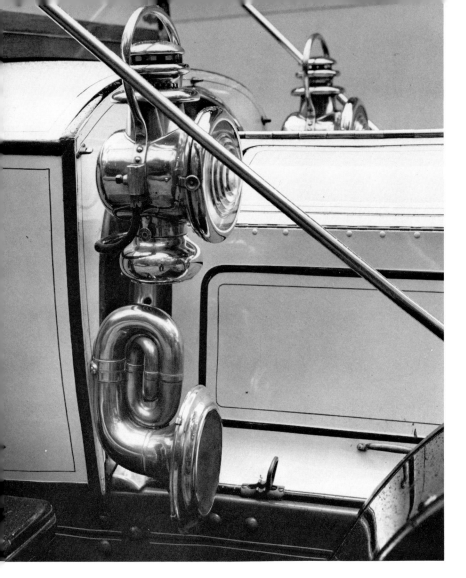

Horn and sidelamp detail of the Packard.

Packard's reputation for rugged construction and reliability was clinched by the remarkable 3500-mile coast-to-coast drive in a mud-caked one-cylinder model dubbed "Old Pacific." This was accomplished in 1903 by Tom Fetch, a sturdy foreman from the Packard factory. What really crowned this achievement was the fact that the previous record, now bettered by three days, had been held by a Winton.

Total production of the one-cylinder Packard was very low; fewer than twelve were made in all of 1900. Production might have continued at this easy pace, had not Henry Bourne Joy entered the scene. Mr. Joy was examining a Packard at the New York Auto Show in 1901 when suddenly the salesman interrupted his sales pitch to leap on the machine and race out of the building in pursuit of a passing fire engine. The fact that one turn of the crank instantly fired up the car so impressed Joy that he later visited the Packard shop in Ohio.

(Left) The heavy steering wheel has a conventional throttle control and spark-advance hand levers. (Right) Two oil-drip sight-feeds are located beneath the gasoline gauge. The box contains the transformer coil for magneto current and a vibrator coil for battery current. The distributor and spark plugs are common to both starting systems.

His interest increased rapidly, leading to large investments in the company by his friends and eventually to the company's move to Detroit.

In the reorganized firm, finally named the Packard Motor Car Company, Joy became an officer and the general manager. He promptly brought Charles Schmidt over from France to spark the engineering section; the most startling result of this move was the production of a 1310-pound racer named the "Grey Wolf." This sleek machine, developing only 24 horsepower, produced a string of upset wins and took fourth place in the Vanderbilt Cup of 1904. Surprisingly enough, an identical production version was listed in the catalogue at $10,000.

(Below) Usually called the "mother-in-law" seat, it was often used by the chauffeur. After the Packard owner and his wife drove to the station or the theater, they would turn the car over to the chauffeur, who would return for them later. (Right) Gear-shift lever and emergency brake are tucked inside, convenient to the driver's right hand. Three forward speeds and one reverse were provided.

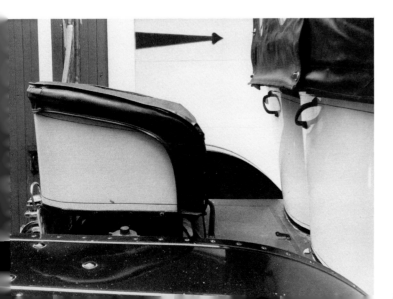

A scaled-down version of the highly successful 30-horsepower engine, the 18 has a bore of 4 1/16 and a stroke of 5⅛ inches. The castings for cylinders, manifolds, and pistons were made in France for Packard from specially adapted gray iron.

After one design disaster, the Model K (made to sell for $7500), Schmidt hit his stride with the Model L. From the shocking sale of only thirty-three Ks, the new Model L rolled out by the hundreds, leading to the 1907 Model 30.

This four-cylinder 30-horsepower machine, created at the urging of Henry Joy, was the right car at the right time. The price range of $4200 to $5700 was for the quality car market, where Joy saw Packard's future. To ensure the widest market without cheapening the product, a smaller model, called the 18 was built. This was virtually a duplicate of the 30 with an appropriately smaller engine. The 1909 Runabout (or touring car), listed for $3200, was made to fill the need for a town or city car, one that did not have the size, power, or roominess needed for long trips.

It is interesting to note that in the period 1909–12, while scores of auto makers were reducing their lines to a few models in order to stay afloat, Packard was doing the opposite. Having built a great demand for the 18, the 30, and their big 48-horsepower six, Packard offered no fewer than thirty-two models in the three series.

Our featured car is a 1911 Model 18, and is variously listed as the "Runabout" or "Gentleman's Speedster" model. Its four-cylinder engine is cast in pairs, with a bore and stroke of 4 1/16 by 5⅛, developing 18 horsepower. The light body is on a wheelbase of 108 inches (4 inches shorter than the Model 18 touring car). The gear box and differential are combined in one housing on the rear

The headlamps were designed for Packard by the leading maker, who engraved that fact proudly and prominently on each brass light.

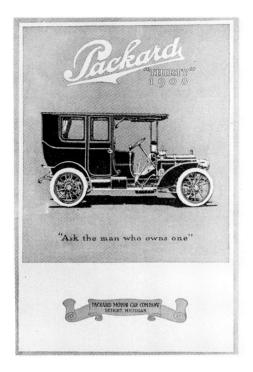

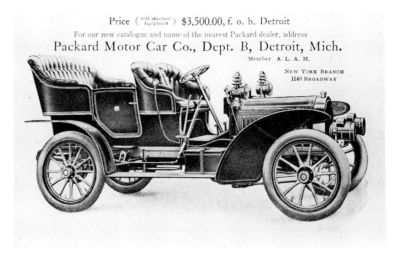

(Left) In contrast to other makers, Packard ads used little text in 1908. This Model 30 limousine rested securely on the company slogan, "Ask the Man Who Owns One." (Above) The four-cylinder Model N, introduced in 1905.

axle. The standard H-pattern gear shift, pioneered in America by Packard, is used. Standard tires for this model are 34 by 4 inches.

The Runabout illustrated was obtained by Norman Viney in 1963 in a partially restored condition. He found various missing parts through other collectors and at the annual Hershey flea market. Mr. Viney was able to locate and restore an original windshield. This device is called the "Packard Stormtilt Windshield," and is hinged at the center to fold outward and down for fair-weather driving. Locating the correct brackets enabled Mr. Viney to transfer the spare tire to the side location, which was optional. A carefully detailed new top completed the restoration.

Although this rare Packard is a high-point machine, the owner delights in driving it on the open road. It cruises comfortably at 40 and will attain 50 mph. Mr. Viney has driven as far as the Greenfield Village car meets, and this 500-mile round trip from Cleveland says much for the reliability that the Packard brothers built into every machine bearing their name.

The huge Solar acetylene gas lamp was the standard headlight for quality cars in 1911.

Completely equipped with top, windshield, speedometer, horn, generator, and lights, the Torpedo Runabout sold for $590.

1912 FORD MODEL T
TORPEDO RUNABOUT

Motor Age Magazine for December, 1915, describes the new features of the forthcoming 1916 models. Referring to Ford, it says, "It is scarcely necessary to go into any lengthy description of the Ford because its general design is well enough known to make that unnecessary ... . Few, if any, other car makers have so designed their chassis in the first place that change was unnecessary for so long a period of time." The unbroken model run that the editor considered so remarkable was seven years old at the time. It was destined to continue until 1927, putting America and the world on wheels.

The Model T was the result of inventor-businessman Henry Ford's growing pains. In the arduous process of trial and error he had tried and failed with several previous models to find the key to automotive success. His first vehicle was crafted in 1896 in a brick shed behind the house he rented on Detroit's Bagley Avenue. The landlord provided the shed for his two tenants to store wood and coal in, but Henry's neighbor became so fascinated by the two-cylinder wonder Ford was constructing that he moved his own fuel supply elsewhere to give the inventor full use of the small building.

Ford was then earning his living as an engineer for the Detroit Edison Company. Shortly after successful runs of his belt-driven car, he was encouraged by Thomas Edison, at a company convention, to press on with his work. After an unsatisfactory involvement with the newly formed Detroit Automobile Company in 1899, Ford formed his own company in 1903. Much has been written about the staggering return on their investments that the dozen original shareholders eventually received. As an example, one hundred dollars put up by James Couzens for his sister earned over a third of a million dollars when she sold out in 1919.

The first production Ford, the original Model A, cost more than a Cadillac and sold well. It was the growing custom to impress the public by racing specially adapted production-line models. In his usual direct way, Ford built two machines solely for speed. Without a conventional transmission, universal joints, or differential, one of these captured the one-mile record mark in 1904 with a speed of 91.4 mph. The bore and stroke of the behemoth 999 was a whopping 7¼

Side detail shows acetylene gas generator fitted to running board.

by 7 inches, providing a piston displacement of 1156 cubic inches. The new company was off to a flying start with an engineer-inventor who was not afraid to take the wheel (or tiller, in this case) of a monster racer onto the frozen reaches of Lake St. Clair and break records.

The new models B and N were moderately successful, and only with the expensive 1905 Model K did Ford finally hit a clinker. The two-speed planetary transmission was not suited to the big heavy six-cylinder car, which caused Ford to approach big machines with extreme caution for decades to come.

The success of the $500 N Runabout led to the launching of the Model T in 1908. It was a success from the first; its faults and foibles were soon known, but sales surged ahead. The tricky transmission caused several states to require a separate driver's license for operators who drove Fords. They may have been hard to start in cold weather and oil hungry, but they were well engineered and incredibly durable.

A rear view of the spidery Model T emphasizes the high road clearance that made it so popular on unimproved back country roads.

(Left) Detail of rear suspension. The multileaved traverse spring, a Ford trademark, was still being used on the Lincoln Continental in 1941. (Right) Looking into the engine room of the Model T.

By 1912, 80,000 T's had been sold, with production soaring to a thousand cars a day the following year. Ford realized the world was eager for a "Universal Car," and he soon had plants in England, France, and Australia, and distributors virtually everywhere.

The ceaseless demand for volume led to the assembly-line techniques that are universally accepted today. At the Highland Park plant moving belts lowered bodies onto a moving chassis line. Ford workers were among the best paid, dating from the startling "five dollars a day" policy announced in 1914. This new minimum rate for "willing workers" was more than double the previous rate.

The price of the Model T was brought lower each year, from a high of $850 to an incredible low of $260. In 1915 Henry Ford made a salesman of every customer by promising a $50 rebate if 300,000 cars were sold in twelve months. That figure was exceeded, and $15 million went back to Ford owners from the company treasury. In the year 1925 over two million were sold.

The Model T became the butt of a thousand jokes and the subject of scores of songs, but the banter was more affectionate than derisive. The car's quirks

The 20-horsepower, four-cylinder engine is cast en bloc with water jacket, upper half of crankcase, and transmission housing an integral unit. Bore and stroke is 3¾ by 4 inches. Over twenty million of these motors were eventually produced.

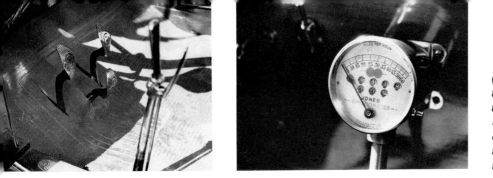

(Far left) Three pedals controlled the planetary gear set. The clutch is at left, reverse in center, and brake at right. (Left) Jones Speedometer is calibrated to an optimistic 60 mph. Top speed of this Ford was under 50 mph.

have left marks on country back roads even today. Turnarounds were frequently cut into the roadside halfway up a steep hill for the benefit of the Tin Lizzie. Low gear couldn't always make it, but reverse gear was lower yet, and many a farmer still remembers crawling up hills in reverse in his faithful Ford.

To earn total sales of over fifteen million, the car had to offer something no other did. People believed it was a quality car and it was; Ford used vanadium steel and pioneered expensive heat-treating techniques long before the rest of the industry. His sales catalogue declared that the car could be lifted in the air by the four fender irons—"the size of your little finger"—because of his super-strength steel. Dealers exhibited axles twisted into corkscrews that had refused to break. The company took great pains to ensure parts availability at low cost, and the car's simple design encouraged the farmer-owner to become his own mechanic.

Almost every maker of cars in the period before World War I offered a semi-racer or runabout. Ford was no exception, and if any Model T can be called sporty, it was the Torpedo Runabout. At $590, it had exactly the same performance as all the other body styles. Top speed was 45 mph, with the 20-horsepower four-cylinder engine delivering as much as thirty miles to the gallon. The car can be entered by a door on either side, an improvement over an earlier Torpedo model without doors.

This Runabout was a popular choice of country doctors, and it was on a doctor's estate in a small Ohio town that the car was discovered in 1958. Since restoration of the vehicle, owner Jack Foreman has shown it in many meets. It took first place of all 1912 makes competing at the 1970 Greenfield Village Antique Car Meet.

The Model T was Henry Ford's favorite brainchild (he even tried retaining the planetary transmission in the Model A!), but his most repeated remark about the car was, "Buy a Ford because it is a better car, not because it is cheaper." Millions of people believed him.

Detail of sidelamp, horn, and louvered hood.

*Built with only 9 inches of ground clearance and a tread of 56 inches, the Mercer
was guaranteed to do the mile in 51 seconds.*

1914 MERCER RACEABOUT
SERIES J, TYPE 35

THERE ARE a handful of cars so steeped in legend that one examines the actual machine in awe. On occasion the reality is a disappointment, and the viewer wonders how the mystique ever developed. Say "Raceabout" to any car buff, however, and "Mercer" will be the immediate response. Scores of machines basically similar in layout and general appearance were built between 1910 and 1915, but few had the combination of performance and almost elegant grace that characterized the 35 J Mercer.

On a chassis that looks like an advanced development of the Orient Buckboard, the Mercer's twin bucket seats nestle low, far back of a dramatically raked dash. The highly crowned fenders are only a few inches lower than the rounded hood that houses the T-head engine. Other than the cowl structure there is literally no body except aft of the huge gas tank, where the twin spares are mounted. The wide 56-inch tread and the long sweep of the front fenders give an impression of length that belies the actual wheelbase measurement of a scant 108 inches. It is a car of flawless proportion that promises high performance by its very appearance. The final elements that made the Mercer legendary were its exceptional speed and remarkable handling.

Before that landmark day in 1910 when Chief Engineer Finley R. Porter decided to design a speedster body around his new four-cylinder, 58-horsepower, T-head powerhouse, the history of the New Jersey car company was typical of scores of other struggling auto plants.

The predecessor of the Mercer Company was the earlier (1906-09) Walter Automobile Company of Trenton, New Jersey. This venture, backed by the wealthy bridge-building Roebling family, seemed unable to settle on a market goal; their models were priced from $3500 to $12,000. The gap between building autos and suspension bridges was considerable, and in 1910 the company was reorganized as the Mercer Automobile Company, taking its name from the county in which it was located. Washington Roebling II, with considerable vision, gave Chief Engineer Porter the go-ahead to design a sporting raceabout.

The resulting swift and nimble machine finished twelfth in the first "Indy" 500 held in May, 1911. The same driver, Hughie Hughes, won three important

The Mercer in profile. Wheelbase, 108 inches; horsepower, 58; top speed, 85 mph.

Stern view of the 35-J Raceabout. Body is built of sheet aluminum.

road races in similar Mercers before the year was out. Engine displacement was the factor for determining class in these events, and the Mercer qualified just within the limit of the 231–300-cubic-inch category. In 1912 Ralph de Palma took a Mercer to the Los Angeles Speedway and ticked off a twenty-mile run at an average speed of 80.5 mph. Hughes returned to the second Indianapolis 500-mile race in 1912 and finished third, despite having the smallest car entered. This combination of a small but potent engine in a car that handled brilliantly was to embarrass the "big boys" once again at Milwaukee later that year when the same driver placed second in the eighth Vanderbilt Cup Race. These non-stock racing machines could qualify for this event with engines up to a whopping 600 cubic inches. Monsters like the 597-c.i. Knox, the 589-c.i. Fiat, and two 590-c.i. Mercedes, trailed the 309-c.i. T-head Mercer, which was barely nosed out of first place by a Mercedes driven by the great de Palma.

The sporting set was much impressed by these achievements at the big races, and many raceabouts were bought solely for the fun of dirt-track competition. The golden age of Porter's rugged T-head lasted just four years, from 1911 to 1914. At $2600 the series 35-J was not inexpensive (raceabouts by Hupp, Buick, Hudson, and others could be had for half that price). Fewer than 500 machines, including tourers, per year were built. Several colors were offered, but canary yellow was the popular choice.

Equal in importance to the outstanding engine was the four-speed gearbox. People who have driven these cars claim they are closer to the modern quick-shifting "four on the floor" than any other non-synchromesh of similar vintage. One car buff who has driven a restored 35-J at 80 mph confided that it was the first machine of that vintage in which he had ever felt reasonably secure. The one exception to complete peace of mind would be the brakes; one has to allow a large stretch of highway to slow down the brute, with its internal expanding shoes on the rear wheels only.

The extremely low bucket seats make steering awkward. The hand pumps are to maintain pressure feed of fuel to the carburetor.

The large gas tank holds 25 gallons of fuel.

The sharply raked dash is sparsely instrumented. Foot rests are affixed to the frame as well as the dash, presumably to keep the driver and his mechanic on board while taking curves at high speed.

Long-legged drivers had a definite advantage in handling the Mercer. Shift lever operates a four-speed transmission mounted on a subframe beneath the floor. Prest-O-Lite tank fuels the huge Dietz acetylene gas headlamps up front.

In 1915 a new era at Mercer was ushered in with left-hand drive and a new L-head engine designed by Erik Delling. The 1700 rpm of the T-head gave way to the 2800 rpm of the new power plant, which was rumored to produce nearly 90 horsepower. Several variations of this model were designed, but wartime production was very low. The Roebling brother who sparked the original raceabout that brought Mercer immortality was lost on the *Titanic*, and in 1918 the last of the three brothers died. Reorganized as Mercer Motors in 1919, the firm produced two more raceabouts, series 4 and 5. These were distinguished by staggered seats and streamlined bodies. At $4675, they were too expensive for the times, although each machine was guaranteed to do 75 mph. The output of the company declined steadily until 1925; nothing but six-cylinder models were made the last two years. Only 135 cars were made in 1925, and then the firm went under. A revival attempt was tried in 1931, of all years, but in that depression-ridden economy it never got beyond the prototype stage.

The restoration of the raceabout illustrated was carried out by a longtime auto enthusiast and authority, Harry B. Johnson, of Reno, Nevada. Over a fifteen-year period he diligently searched out and acquired missing parts, taking care to use only authentic and original components. While most surviving 35-J's have wooden spoked wheels, the wire wheels shown are correct and were an original option. The car is now on display in the outstanding collection of Harry Resnick at the Motor Museum in Ellenville, New York.

When a car buff, spying a weed-choked old barn guarded by a rusty padlock, feverishly peers through the grimy window in the side wall, chances are one car leads all others in his hoped-for discovery—the Mercer. No other machine has ever captured so well the discovery of motoring as this lean and hungry brass-trimmed beauty.

Rudge-Whitworth wire wheels were an original option and carry 32 by 4½ tires.

The Mercer Raceabout at the 1968 Parke-Bernet auction, where it was bought by the Motor Museum of Ellenville, New York.

The glass monocle wind-shield, an optional accessory, gave scant protection at high speed.

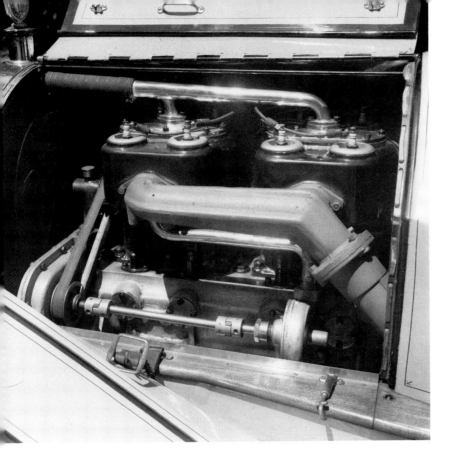

The 58-horsepower T-head four-cylinder engine. Displacement is 298 cubic inches with a bore and stroke of 4½ by 5 inches.

The passenger's view down the road touring in the Mercer. Goggles are a must for riders in this low-slung, wide-open machine.

1913 AUSTRO-DAIMLER
PRINCE HENRY ROADSTER
Body by Healy of New York

THE STORY behind this advanced and potent performer goes back to the very infancy of the automobile. The firm of Austro-Daimler was incorporated in Vienna in 1899 to provide local production of one hundred Daimler cars a year for the Austrian market. These machines were duplicates of the 4-cylinder model made by the parent Daimler plant in Cannstadt, Germany.

Although American production techniques were moving ahead rapidly, most of our domestic engines were of one- and two-cylinder design. It may surprise some, but by the turn of the century, Gottlieb Daimler and his associate, Wilhelm Maybach, had been perfecting internal-combustion engine design in Germany for almost nineteen years. When Ferdinand Porsche was hired as director of the Austro-Daimler plant in 1906, the multicylinder engine employing the atomizing carburetor was already well established in Europe.

Porsche had earned a reputation as a daring innovator for his Jules Verne-like "Elektromobil," built for the Lohner Company in 1900. This strange vehicle sported a curved dash that resembled a huge seashell; and a monster cyclops headlamp lit the road ahead. The bulging hubs of the front wheels concealed twin 80-volt electric motors developing about 5 horsepower and weighing 250 pounds each.

Although Porsche personally drove a stripped version of this machine to victory in a local race against gas-powered competition, he quickly realized that a car with a range limited to fifty miles before battery depletion had poor prospects. He then tried what has been sought ever since as a logical solution: a gasoline engine driving generator to power one or more electric motors. The resulting vehicle, which was called, logically enough, the "Mixt," performed remarkably. Deciding that the rear wheels should also contribute something, Porsche promptly created a version with an electric motor in all four wheel hubs. Sustained speeds of over 70 mph were attained, which was unheard of for an electrically powered vehicle. Porsche not only designed and supervised the construction of his unorthodox machines, he also drove them brilliantly to victory after victory.

(Opposite) The Prince Henry Roadster in a setting reminiscent of the Franz Joseph era. (Photography by permission of the Frederick C. Crawford Auto-Aviation Museum, Western Reserve Historical Society, Cleveland, Ohio.)

The pointed radiator was a distinctive Austro-Daimler trademark in the firm's early years. This custom body was built by the Healy Company of New York.

In his new role at Austro-Daimler, Porsche replaced Daimler's son Paul. The firm's 1909 offerings were T-head four-cylinder machines driven, at the customer's choice, by either live-axle or chain drive. It was in 1910, faced with the challenge of winning the important Prince Henry trials of that year, that Porsche created the auto destined to elevate Austro-Daimler to the top rank of contemporary racing machines. The four-cylinder engine he designed produced 86 horsepower at 1400 rpm. The relatively light chassis of 2000 pounds enabled a top speed in excess of 85 mph. This 5.6-liter power plant used individually cast cylinders, each having a steel liner. It was a single overhead camshaft design with one large inlet valve and four exhaust valves per cylinder. Initially propelled by the ever-dependable chains, later versions had shaft drive.

The Prince Henry trials of 1910 arrived on a warm June day, and the competition was top notch, including such vehicles as Pomeroy's Vauxhall. More than a hundred cars participated, but the three light and powerful Porsche creations swept the field, taking first, second, and third place. The Austro-Daimler win

(Opposite) The unique combination of a monocle windshield and a conventional opening give a bizarre front-end appearance to the Austro-Daimler.

The massive look of the rear belies the actual chassis weight of only 2000 pounds.

Shift and brake levers were carried outside the boat-like Healy body. Note the extreme rake of the steering wheel.

created a strong demand for the new car. Most of the Austro-Daimlers produced between 1910 and 1914 were bodied in the popular tulip style, in which the car sides flare out from the running boards in a shape reminiscent of that flower.

The "Prince Henry" pictured is unusual in that it was custom bodied in New York City by the Healy firm. Described either as a three-passenger roadster or as a "cloverleaf" style, it has one thronelike seat behind the twin bucket seats up front. The stern is rounded in an early version of boattail roadsters to come. Commodore Vanderbilt is thought to have been the car's original owner. The machine was purchased for the Frederick C. Crawford Auto-Aviation Museum in 1952 at the Cameron Peck auction. Remarkably well preserved, it has been one of the museum's most popular exhibits ever since.

The Austro-Daimler firm went on to produce other fine cars, notably the 100-mph Type ADM built in the midtwenties and employing an aluminum six-cylinder engine of 115 hp. The other great design Porsche created for the company was the 1932 "Bergmeister" with its outstanding suspension system. As its name, "mountain master," implied, it was designed for swift Alpine touring or racing. Its success led to the overly ambitious ADR eight-cylinder, intended to be the last word in mountain climbing for the Ritz-Carlton crowd. As in America, the European social set of 1933 was staying away from luxury auto salesrooms in droves, and Austro-Daimler hurriedly merged with the Steyr Company. Auto production ceased around 1934 after the combine of Austro-Daimler, Steyr, and Puch was created.

Ferdinand Porsche had earlier, in 1923, gone to the parent Daimler company in Germany as director of engineering. He later put Steyr on the automotive map with the brilliantly conceived and executed 100-horsepower straight-eight "Austria" in 1929. In 1931, he formed his own design firm. Porsche's creations have ranged from the prototype of the Volkswagen to the 80-ton "Tiger" tanks of the German army. His accomplishments cover an extraordinary range during the most creative period in automotive history. The Prince Henry, one of his least known achievements, is nevertheless one of the most worthy.

The Porsche-designed four-cylinder engine produces 86 horsepower at 1400 rpm. It has an overhead camshaft and uses individually cast cylinders with steel liners.

Superb manufacturing standards were set for the Porsche engine. The fan is a single massive casting.

Instruments are buried under a very deep cowl in the Prince Henry. Pedal arrangement is unusual; left pedal is the clutch, right is the throttle, and two middle pedals are both brakes that act independently on separate drums of the rear transmission.

(Left) The lever below the monocle windshield controls air and gas mixture. (Right) Custom body plate of the Healy Company.

Rear seat of the three-passenger Healy-designed body. Storage lockers take the place of usual trunk.

An amalgamation of varied Model T components successfully combined into a Ford Speedster.

1915 FORD MODEL T
SPEEDSTER

IT SHOULD be stated immediately that Ford built no true production speedster or raceabout-bodied Model T's. It must be admitted that even the year designation of this barn-built Ford is arbitrary. Model T experts will spot the fenders as dating from 1911 and the running gear from a 1924 chassis. The owner-builder of this machine has merely done recently what Ford enthusiasts have been doing ever since the Model T appeared on the market in 1908, namely, making the Lizzie look fast and sporty. The early tinkerers should be divided into two groups, really. There were those who made major mechanical improvements to engine, suspension, and body. They sought to convert the Humble Ford into a real dirt-track racer, and many of them achieved startling results. Others were content to work with an unchanged chassis and create a dashing-looking raceabout that still delivered the modest factory performance of every other T.

A typical project to build a real performer out of a T usually followed these lines: buy a factory-new chassis, which was offered by Ford from the first for those customers who built special-purpose bodies. Remove the fenders, running boards, and windshield. The engine was "hotted up" by machining off the cylinder head to raise the compression. Double springs were put on all valves, and a Bosch magneto with advanced timing was installed. The steering was raked to fit the lower seat. The gas tank was placed behind rather than under the seat to lower the silhouette. A new body, usually of aluminum, was fitted. The top speed of the 20-horsepower car, previously 45 mph, might now be in the neighborhood of 75 mph. This usually demanded suspension changes, because the bouncy traverse springs made the vehicle uncontrollable at high speed. At least one example I have seen solved this problem by turning the back axle over and converting the chassis to an underslung design.

Overhead valves and raised compression gave some of these custom-built racers amazing performance. Noel Bullock, a famed dirt-track race driver of the twenties, left more powerful cars far behind in his Ford racer during the grueling Pike's Peak Hill Climb of 1922.

The appeal of these home-built racers lay in the ready supply of cheap cars and parts. In the thirties a running T might be found almost anywhere for

Careful workmanship and an eye for proportion distinguish this home-built machine.

five to twenty dollars. I recall a high-school friend driving up one Saturday morning in 1941 in a well-preserved touring Ford T he had just purchased for five dollars! The incident has remained engraved in my mind because, while several of us were discussing the vehicle, it suddenly slipped into gear and chugged off. The new owner finally overtook it after a three-block sprint that must have topped some local records, had it been timed.

For those early T owners who wanted only the dashing look of a junior Mercer Raceabout, the route was much simpler. Starting with a cut-down body or no body at all, they installed the most suitable bucket seats they could find. Dozens of firms supplied kits or even complete bodies for simplified installation on the buyer's chassis. These were usually wood-framed, aluminum-covered creations sporting such names as the "Cyclone" or "Greyhound Speedster." Available in several colors and with fully upholstered seats, they cost about seventy-five dollars, complete with tool box and gas tank.

Mr. Foreman, who built the speedster illustrated, acquired a dilapidated 1924 Model T Tourer from a barn in Rudolf, Ohio. Considering its poor condition, he decided to create a speedster instead of attempting a conventional restoration. He rebuilt the 1924 engine and installed it in an older Model T frame. The hood is from an early model and the differential from the very last 1927 model. The radiator dates from the 1910–14 production, and the wheels from 1923 to 1925. The fenders are modern reproductions of the 1911 style. The gas tank is a commercial 20-gallon industrial drum with baffle plates installed to prevent the fuel from sloshing.

Mr. Foreman patterned the car's general layout after a speedster in the Ford Museum at Dearborn. The auto runs comfortably at 35 mph and is driven frequently in local parades. The owner notes that the recent increased availability of reproduction parts for Model T's has greatly simplified the undertaking of a Ford speedster project. Although they are not restorations in the true sense of the word, they are a true reflection of a period when the self-taught mechanic wasn't afraid to "build his own."

Cap gracing early Model T radiator is from an Overland.

Fenders are modern reproductions of correct 1911 design.

Slanted cowl and monocle windshield are details styled after raceabouts of the Mercer era.

(Above) The horn bulb is convenient to the driver's left hand. (Right) Detail of the roomy cockpit.

(Left) The familiar 20-horsepower four-cylinder engine is a 1924 model; it was completely rebuilt by Mr. Foreman. (Below) The bright red speedster has won awards in local Ohio old-car meets and is a dependable parade car.

6. THE CLASSIC ERA

CERTAIN basic criteria apply to all automobiles with any claim to classic status. Such cars were usually the top effort of their maker and hence were among the most expensive models that the car-builder offered. This almost automatically excludes those firms devoted solely to low-priced cars. Classics are distinguished by outstanding engineering or coachwork, or both. In the category of great cars with sporting characteristics, another significant factor enters: classic sports vehicles were innovative. If one considers a Packard roadster and a Stutz roadster from the late twenties, one would have to concede that the Stutz has the edge in original engineering. This is not to minimize the engineering standards of Packard, but to give credit for the advanced thinking that so often found expression in sports models.

Packard itself proved this point when it introduced the Speedster series in 1930, with the stunning Model 734 boattail roadster as the line leader. Producing this highly tuned 145-horsepower gem indicated that the staid firm realized it had been a long time since the legend of the Grey Wolf had filled salesrooms with customers. It is not known how much money Packard made selling only 150 of these beauties at $5210 per copy, but the aura of brilliance that the 734 Speedster added to the entire 1930 Packard line is indisputable.

Of the criteria of engineering innovation, brilliant body design, engineering quality, limited production, outstanding performance, and high original cost, the last is probably least significant. The factory-body Auburn boattails of 1932–36 were surprisingly low priced for their time and for what they offered.

The Classic Car Club of America has established an approved roster of autos having classic status. There are omissions of fine makes that should perhaps be included, but it is a sound roll call. One thing is certain, however; as time passes, other great cars of the decades after World War II will be collected. Many of these superb machines are already referred to as classics, and efforts will be made by one group or another to keep adding cars to the accepted pantheon of greats. The peak that the auto industry attained in the twenties and early thirties can never be revisited, however. Cars may be faster, last longer, and ride more smoothly and quietly, but never again will the combination of brilliant engineering and the infinite variety of superb custom body-building be available at any price.

(Opposite) The grille of this 1932 Marmon V-16 symbolizes the classic car era.

The 1923 Stutz. The catalogue fails to list or illustrate bumpers as optional equipment. At this time many sports models were driven without their protection.

1923 STUTZ SPEEDWAY MODEL ROADSTER

MANY EARLY car makers raced their machines because they believed the public would buy "winners." Henry Ford, James Packard, and others in those exciting years of dynamic competition knew it was smart business to offer their customers production autos that reflected the glamour of triumph on the banked curves of the speedway.

The Stutz auto went beyond racing as a sales aid. From the beginning the company stressed that the Stutz sold to the public was the same machine that was being raced. Mercer was not the only sports-bodied car being driven straight from the salesroom to the dirt track; in the years just before World War I those classic raceabouts were frequently competing against Stutz Bear-Cats. This early concern for speed, reliability, and handling was later reflected in what could well be called the first production "safety car," the New Stutz for 1926.

Harry C. Stutz was born and raised on a small Ohio farm. He was more interested in repairing and improving farm machinery than in raising crops, and he eventually arrived on the Indianapolis automotive scene after an automotive seasoning period of nine years in Dayton, Ohio.

In the years between 1903 and 1910, when he formed his own company, Stutz displayed an outstanding gift for engineering. He designed the very advanced underslung chassis for the American Motor Car Company in 1905. His early recognition of the importance of a low center of gravity in auto design was fully developed by his company twenty years later in the remarkable "Safety Chassis" model of 1926.

Shortly after Stutz's company got off to a well-financed start, they decided to enter a car in the first Indianapolis 500, an event the whole country awaited. Barely two weeks before the 1911 race, the first fully Stutz-designed car was completed and delivered to the track. It placed eleventh in the big race, just out of the money, but the Stutz-designed unitized transmission and rear axle performed flawlessly. It was a good showing for a brand-new auto and led to the slogan, "The Car that Made Good in a Day." Catalogue writers in 1922 were still referring to this event in glowing, if inaccurate, terms. In their copy,

The car is painted Royal Red, with fenders and lower body finished in black.

The Speedway Model Roadster is distinguished from the Bearcat by its longer wheelbase (130 inches instead of 120 inches) and by having doors.

the ad men reduced the 500 miles to 300 and claimed a Stutz had placed "in the money." No matter, the car and the man soon shared a reputation for the highest standards of integrity and quality.

In the following years Stutz entered event after event. This was the golden age of road races, some as short as the eight-mile Fairmount Park event in Philadelphia, some as long as the two- and three-hundred-mile races at Cincinnati and Santa Monica. The two crack drivers of the Stutz banner, Gil Anderson and Earl Cooper, took on all contenders and made their car nationally known. The opposition usually were Europe's best cars, whose drivers sat behind power plants that dwarfed the Stutz engines.

In 1915, after a number of important wins, including Barney Oldfield's epic run in a Stutz in the Cactus Derby (a choking grind over mountain and desert from Los Angeles to Phoenix), the company capitalized on their track reputation and concentrated on passenger car production.

The outstanding performance of the Bear-Cat (hyphenated in factory brochures) in every type of competition brought in the customers from the beginning. It was no svelte semi-racer, but looked more like a high-riding, stripped-down tourer. Its wheelbase of 120 inches was long, and its 389-cubic inch, 60-horsepower, four-cylinder engine delivered its thrust to the rear wheels via a novel transaxle. Not as fast as the Mercer (it weighed 1000 pounds more), the Bear-Cat was a close match and scores of dirt-track sprints were held by champions of both makes.

Production of the Stutz was never a flood, a total of 2207 being made in 1917. The car evolved steadily, with an enlarged four-cylinder and a six added. The big seller in 1922 was still the 16-valve, T-head four-cylinder, with a bore and stroke of 4⅜ by 6 inches.

It is interesting to note that at a time when other makers were cutting costs to ensure a maximum flow of cars out the plant gate, Stutz was doing some things only Rolls or Duesenberg could match: every completed chassis was fitted with factory wheels and a test body and given a thorough test on the road. After passing this critical inspection, the production body was installed, and each car was again road tested. It should be remembered that Stutz was never a cheap car, although its quality made it seem relatively inexpensive. The Stutz eight-cylinder of 1926 at $3295 was $300 more than the Cadillac V-8 and $700 more than Packard's straight eight of that year.

In 1919 Harry Stutz had bowed out of the company he founded and formed H.C.S. to produce a new car under that name. The original Stutz Company was now in the hands of bankers and financiers and might have collapsed in short order but for the providential appointment in 1924 of Fred Moskovics as president. The new executive was a unique combination of superlative manag-

Graceful lines and left-hand drive are evident in this view of the 1923 Stutz. The make was offered with right-hand drive until 1922.

Custom-design trunk is fitted in factory spare-wheel well, with dual spares carried over the gas tank.

er and all-around technical wizard. Under his leadership, the company launched a great new engine, the vertical eight, in the "Safety Chassis" New Stutz. This imaginative design allowed lowering the floor of the car by five inches without sacrificing adequate road clearance. Brewster, noted custom body builder, supervised design and construction of the new bodies for Stutz. The windshield was of safety glass, the running boards were of reinforced steel to act as side barriers in a collision, and novel "hydrostatic" four-wheel brakes were standard. The car was very well received, and 1926 production was 3700.

Losing the famed 1928 match race at Indy with a Hispano-Suiza was a disappointment to the company, but was partly compensated for by the stirring battle one privately entered Stutz Black Hawk gave the vaunted Bentley

Tread of the Stutz is the same as Mercer's, 56 inches. Brakes are huge 16-inch drums.

Front axle is drop forged and has oversized steering knuckles equipped with roller bearings.

Factory team of five cars at the 1928 Le Mans race, losing to the sole surviving Bentley by an eyelash.

Fred Moskovics left Stutz in 1929, but the engineering team he left behind weathered the depression for one last fling. Still based on the same chassis and the vertical-eight engine, the new Bear-Cat showed a remarkable increase in power, considering the lean engineering budget. Twin overhead camshafts, four valves per cylinder, and a single spark plug in each hemi-head cylinder worked wonders; the Bearcat carrying this DV-32 engine was guaranteed to do 100 mph. In the soup-line days of 1932, few people cared about going anywhere at 100 mph, and only 700 cars were made between 1930 and the 1937 petition for bankruptcy.

Today, collectors' favorites are undoubtedly the early and late Bearcats, as well as those few cars fitted with custom bodies. The 1923 Stutz illustrated is a Speedway Model Roadster and is authentically restored except for the custom trunk, designed to fit in the spare wheel well. Andrew Adler purchased

(Left) Taillamp and stoplight are in one unit. (Right) Hub of wire wheels, which were standard equipment.

English walnut sections are fastened to the 18-inch aluminum steering wheel. Gas and spark levers are conventional in design.

the car in Texas in a partially restored condition. He has continued to improve the Stutz, which has taken several trophies. Mr. Adler describes the car's handling as being on the heavy side, with remarkable acceleration from the 389-cubic-inch engine.

Reading a sales catalogue of 1922, you will find that the very equipment list conjures up visions of cruising in a new Stutz over those uncrowded dirt or gravel roads of the twenties. Your machine is trimmed in black and nickel, painted Royal Red or Elephant Gray; your searchlight is at hand on the Special "rain-vision" windshield post. The "Neverleek" top will keep you dry no matter what the elements, the Boyce Motometer up front tells you all is well under that gleaming hood. Your Hartford shocks deftly soak up every rut as the dial on your speedometer spins into the seventies. After your exhilarating run, you guide your Stutz into the barn, brush a speck of dust from the Spanish Blue (hand-buffed) upholstery, and retire to count your blessings.

How much of old-car magic is nostalgia and how much is plain mechanical fun is hard to determine. Behind the wheel of this Stutz Roadster, it becomes a very academic question.

Walnut dash displays standard instruments, including Delco dual ignition and 75 mph speedometer.

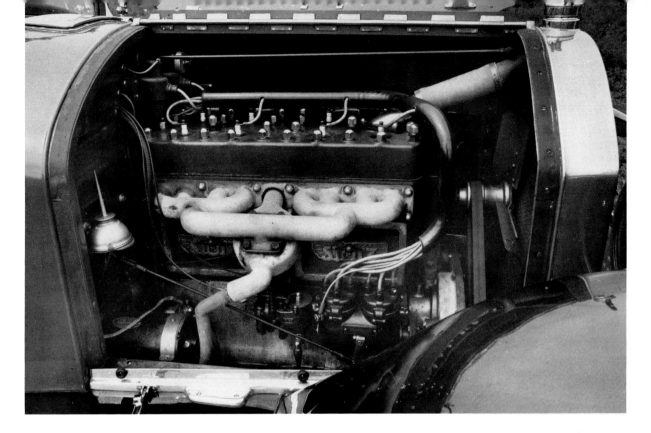

Intake side of the 16-valve, four-cylinder Stutz motor. It has an aluminum alloy crankcase and features forced-feed lubrication through a hollow crankshaft.

Exhaust side of the big 4⅜ by 6 T-head engine.

Boyce Motometer on filler cap was standard equipment.

The touring model Speedway Four, offered in 1923.

The **STuTZ** Speedway Four

1926 LINCOLN V-8
BOATTAIL ROADSTER
Body by Brunn

IN THE rapidly changing technology of the early automotive age, bright young men could become expert in many of the new technical disciplines by their twenties or thirties. For this reason many of the founders of the several hundred auto companies that were created up to the time of World War I were young men. But in 1920, at the age of seventy-seven, Henry M. Leland formed the Lincoln Motor Company. He named his car for an illustrious President, a man he had actually voted for in the distant days of his youth.

Leland had already carved out a career as one of the half dozen top leaders on the American automobile scene. He had engineered the engine of the curved-dash Olds back in 1901 and had risen to head the Cadillac Company. During the war he produced over 6,000 Liberty aircraft engines.

The new Lincoln produced in 1921 was a V-8 powered car. The engine was quite different from the V-8 design Leland had produced at Cadillac back in 1914, however. The new power plant had its twin banks of four cylinders inclined at a 60-degree angle, rather than 90 degrees, as in the Cadillac. The most novel feature, which was very expensive to manufacture, was the "fork and blade" connecting rod. The owner's manual cautioned the purchaser that "the forked rod and crank pin bearing which it contains must never be adjusted." The remedy for wear was a new bearing. The engine ran on five main crankshaft bearings and was the most precisely machined and balanced engine of the time. It displaced 358 cubic inches and was rated at a modest 81 horsepower.

The chassis beneath this superb engine was equally well engineered. Unfortunately, buyers were not all appreciative engineers and were turned off by the prosaic, boxlike, ho-hum body designs offered. The public reacted as if it had been invited to a Rembrandt exhibit and been shown paint-by-numbers pictures.

With apathy at the showrooms and booming production costs because of Leland's fanatical standards of perfection, the government chose this moment to hit the company with a back-tax bill of almost five million dollars for alleged

(Opposite) The clean lines of the Lincoln grille blend with the graceful shape of the Brunn body.

Massive chassis is evident. Ribbed lines on headlight lenses match vertical grille louvers.

Two wheelbase lengths were offered, this 130-inch chassis and one of 136 inches for the large touring models.

profits on the wartime Liberty engine project. The company had inadequate capital to weather the storm until sales picked up, so the receivers took over. When the Lincoln Motor Company was put on the block, Henry Ford stepped in and bought it for eight million dollars. A bitter period of charges and countercharges followed, with Leland convinced that Ford had misled him as to his continuing in charge of operations. The result was the resignation of Leland, Senior, and his son Wilfred a few months later.

Perhaps the best tribute Ford could pay to the man who had taken his place at Cadillac many years before was to continue the Lincoln chassis virtually unchanged. With Edsel Ford taking a major role, top body designers were brought in to create coachwork worthy of the great engineering that lay hidden beneath. Judkins, Brunn, Willoughby, and Locke were among those whose designs would bring Lincoln to the top ranks of America's prestige cars.

For ten years the Lincoln continued to be more Leland than Ford. The engine acquired aluminum pistons and improved manifolds and climbed from 81 to 120 horsepower. Until it was replaced in 1932, the L engine still meant Leland design in a Ford production to many people.

Had the factory first considered a production design like the Brunn-built custom illustrated here, Leland might have had the orders to stave off his creditors. Oddly enough, few sporting-type bodies were made for Lincolns at any time. This Brunn creation of 1926 was ordered by William Pierce Hamilton III, of Bar Harbor, Maine. He owned the car until 1938 and was usually a passenger, his chauffeur driving. The snug cockpit makes it a most unusual choice for a chauffeur-driven vehicle, but who could resist the daring—for 1926—boattail styling? The car was later the property of a retired Bar Harbor sea captain, and there it stayed in storage until advertised for sale in 1956. Robert Wells was the fortunate buyer, obtaining both the Brunn-bodied auto and a 1926 factory-bodied Lincoln roadster. The price scale of 15 years ago can bring tears to the eyes of today's collector. Let it simply be said that in that same column of *The New York Times* a 1937 Cord 812 supercharged phaeton in fine condition was offered for $1250!

Mr. Wells had his find shipped to his Akron, Ohio, home and began restoration. The car was not running, because the block was cracked. A new one was installed, and the low-mileage auto needed little other mechanical attention. The body proved to be aluminum with steel fenders. It was determined that Brunn had lowered the top six inches. A new windshield was fitted, and the missing bows replaced. Fortunately, the original greyhound and headlamps were intact. The car now rides on new 700 by 21 tires. Despite its sporty look, this Lincoln weighs 4700 pounds. It can be started in high gear and takes steep hills easily in top gear. Both Mr. and Mrs. Wells drive the car and both find that the

The boattail rear-end design by Brunn. The reduced height of the top adds to the car's sporty look.

(Above) Three-quarter view of the Lincoln. (Below) No armrests are provided in the one-passenger rumble seat of this custom Lincoln.

The Leland V-8 engine. With a bore and stroke of 3⅜ by 5 inches, it displaces 358 cubic inches. It was rated at 81 horsepower, but actual output is nearer 90 at 2800 rpm.

steering is heavy and that the brakes demand a strong foot. The V-8 moves it along at a comfortable cruising speed of 55 mph.

Production of the Lincoln was up to about 8000 cars yearly in the midtwenties, with the total run for the decade amounting to just over 65,000 vehicles. Four-wheel brakes became standard in 1927, but Henry Ford was content to continue the Lincoln as his prestige "loss-leader" showpiece almost unchanged otherwise until 1932. Then, with Pierce, Marmon, Packard, and, of course, Cadillac all in the multicylinder race, Ford revived the Lincoln with a new 448-cubic-inch V-12 engine. The quick way to determine if you have discovered one of these gems, called the KB Model, is to check the wheelbase; the 145-inch chassis was reserved for this engine alone. I recently drove six hours to see if a Lincoln moldering under wraps in an Ohio barn was, indeed, a rare KB. Alas, it proved to be a 1933 KA, the smaller V-12, in a factory-bodied sedan on the shorter 136-inch wheelbase.

From 1934 until the end of the classic series, a new version of the V-12, a 414-cubic-inch engine producing 150 horses, powered all Lincolns. These K Lincolns were dropped just before the war, and the Zephyr and Continental line carried the Lincoln name until the postwar period. It is strictly a personal opinion, but of all the recent Ford products that have borne the Lincoln name, I can imagine Henry Leland most impressed with the series that began in 1961 and ended in 1965. They were engineered and quality built far beyond the prevailing indstry standards and coupled outstanding performance with timeless styling.

The Lincoln as found in storage in 1956. Car was in primer and had a cracked block.

"Fat man" or swing-away steering wheel was a useful option in cramped cockpit of Lincoln.

Hub of Lincoln wire wheel.

No roadster of the twenties was considered complete without a searchlight mounted on the windshield post.

The attractive dash is highly polished metal with the normal complement of instruments.

Brunn & Company, custom body builder of Buffalo, New York, built this aluminum-bodied sports model for Lincoln.

(Left) A Locke-bodied 1926 Lincoln roadster with side-mounts. (Above) A 1927 sport touring model on the longer wheelbase chassis.

1928 PACKARD RUNABOUT
MODEL 533

THIS Packard roadster was the last of the big sixes that the company made; not until 1937 was a six offered to the public again. Management realized in the twenties that the day of bigger engines was here to stay and planned accordingly. Packard had introduced an outstanding eight in 1923 and was able to expand this series easily. Other makers, Pierce Arrow for example, had failed to gauge the public demand correctly and carried their outdated six-cylinder engine long after its sales appeal had evaporated. Packard also had the reputation garnered by the brilliant twin six it had marketed during the war years.

This runabout is by no means a small car. Built on a wheelbase of 133 inches, it weighs 3700 pounds. When dozens of other sixes and many eights were available in 1928 for under $1500, this Packard model cost over $2000. Its Single Six engine has a bore and stroke of 3½ by 5 inches and produces 82 horsepower. Over 50,000 Packards were sold in this banner year, most of them the Model 526 and 533 six-cylinder machines.

Alex Bell found his runabout in Willington, Ohio, through a friend's tip. It presented a sorry appearance, with the right rear fender missing, as was the top and virtually all the upholstery. The battery had long since expired, so the car could not be started. An effort to pull the car home with a tow bar was unsuccessful because the Packard refused to turn corners with the towing vehicle. The weather was extremely cold, and despite the lack of a top, Mr. Bell took the wheel behind a tow rope and endeavored to guide the reluctant machine home. After completing one leg of the trip as far as Columbus (and losing his hat to the wind in the process), the new owner decided a delay was more acceptable than pneumonia, and sent a farm-implement truck to haul the roadster the rest of the way home to Ottawa, Ohio.

Restoration, which took about a year, was aided by locating and purchasing a series-533 sedan parts car in Daneville, Ohio. Flea markets were scoured from Indiana to Hershey, Pennsylvania, for missing parts. A Toledo foundry cast some parts, and mechanical restoration and painting was completed in Mr. Bell's home town. The car is regularly driven to regional meets and parades.

(Opposite) Packard's factory body styles for their roadsters and phaetons were extremely stylish.

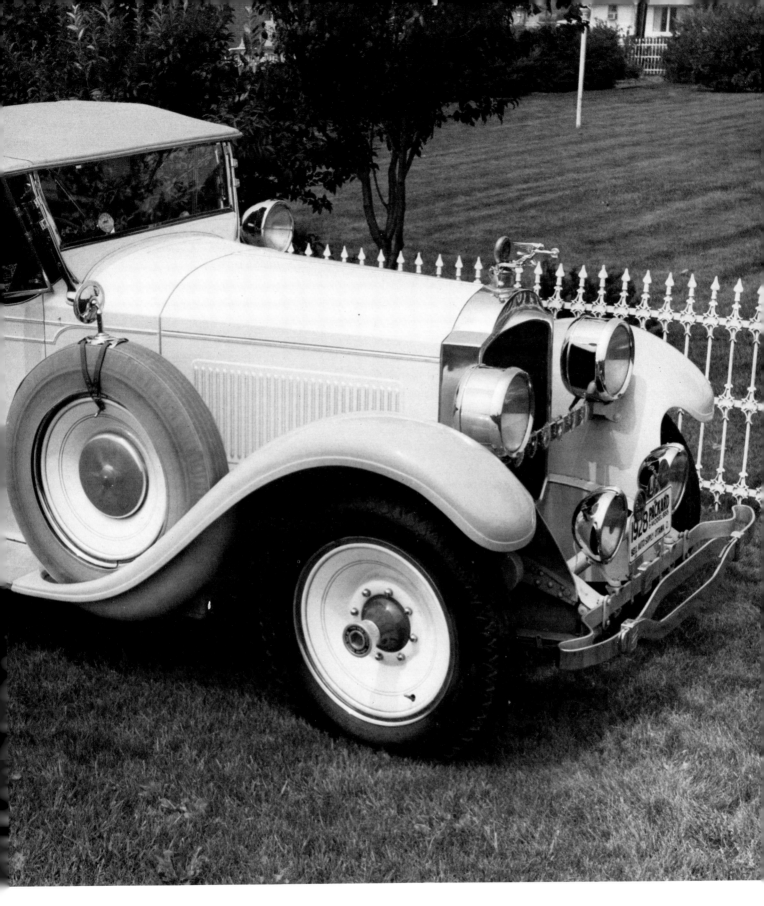

Drum headlights and disc wheels are features of the big Packard series 533.

Rear view of the big runabout.

Cockpit of the 533. Note rakish windwings and storage pockets in doors.

(Left) Carpet and auxiliary amp meter below dash are only nonoriginal items. (Below) The last refinement of the Packard big six has a bore and stroke of 3½ by 5 and develops 82 horespower.

130

(Above) Detail of the massive trunk and rack, which was optional equipment on the 1928 car. (Below) Detail featuring combined taillight and stoplight. Trunk rack option required special bumper.

(Above) Suspension detail on Packard front end. (Below) Running board spotlight is finishing detail for an outstanding restoration.

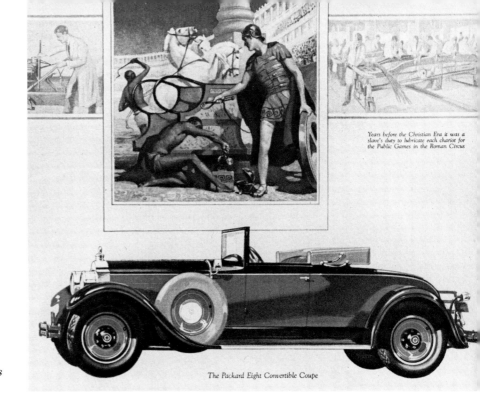

The Packard Eight Convertible Coupe

Packard stressed craftsmanship in this famous series of ads in 1928.

"It drives like a Mack truck, but the pleasure of sharing its beauty with others makes it all worthwhile," the owner says.

Packard entered the thirties in sound condition, and the depression did not prevent the company from building a sizable number of truly great autos. The Super Eight and the new V-12 of 1932, all with beautiful factory bodies or custom coachwork, have become the most sought after of American classics. While other companies folded in the mid-depression stretch, Packard survived by making low-priced cars that carried their name, prestige, and famed grille. Whether this was a sound decision has been hotly debated; actually, it was the only way to stay in business.

The postwar operation of the company left a lot to be desired. The public has always been impatient for perfection; let one flaw appear in a newly designed car, and the entire concept is rejected. The last true Packard, the 1956 line, was the equal of them all and superior to most other American production cars of the time. But bugs in the very advanced suspension system and a bad lot of axle shafts in early models caused the public to stay away permanently.

When the Avanti was launched in 1962, the Studebaker-Packard Corporation seriously considered naming it Packard. New generations of car buffs have only to view the surviving great motor cars Packard built in their salad days to understand the undying prestige that name will always have for millions of people.

Rounded headlights have replaced drums, and lines are more flowing in this 1928 dual-cowl phaeton model Packard.

Open coachwork and cycle fenders reveal the superb construction and low-slung design of this Mercedes Benz SS tourer. The immense brake drums were copper plated to speed dissipation of heat.

1929 MERCEDES-BENZ SS

THERE ARE fast cars of elegant grace, and then there are the rugged four-wheeled machines that seem to exude a feeling of sheer brute power and speed. During the six years from 1924 until 1930, Mercedes-Benz produced a classic series of sports models in the latter catagory called the Ks; the K stood for Kompressor, or supercharger. Three sizes of Roots-type blowers were used to raise output for brief periods. (Roots, incidentally, refers to a Connersville, Indiana, firm that pioneered in this field.) This series of cars, with a dazzling and confusing array of model designations, swept the field of European racing events into the early thirties.

The basic K was a six-cylinder design that produced 110 horsepower at 2800 rpm and leaped to 160 horsepower with the supercharger cut in. Many parts were made of a light alloy, and engine lubrication and cooling were unusually efficient in this Porsche-designed motor. The car's frame was conventional and heavily braced. With a Mercedes factory body, the K was not striking or unusual in appearance, just impressive in its Germanic way, by virtue of its outstanding craftsmanship. The price was impressive, too, well over $5000.

The same single-overhead-cam six-cylinder was continued into the later S and SSK series. Some few details might help to convey the attention to perfection that Porsche always gave. The block and crankcase were a one-piece casting of a strong light alloy. Finish and fitting of these engines was so precise that the lightweight oil sump was fastened directly to the crankcase, with the machining of both surfaces so accurate that an oil-tight seal was obtained without the usual gasket. Many of the engine accessories were beautifully "engine turned."

The running gear of the K was incredibly strong. Universal joints and the rear-end gears were far larger and heavier than current practice dictated. The mechanical brakes could be adjusted by handwheels from the driver's seat. The huge drums were effective but took herculean effort to apply. Some early models were wisely fitted with Bosch vacuum-assist power brakes.

In 1927 the S model appeared, and this 180-horsepower version took the first three places in the Nuerburgring Grand Prix of Germany. In 1928, Rudolf Caracciola in an SSK took first in this event, and was followed by two more SS models for another Mercedes sweep. Scores of other wins, from hill climbs to road races, in Belgium, Ireland, Germany, and Monaco followed.

Detail of huge exhaust pipes that identify all S series Mercedes.

This body style, without doors, is described as a close-coupled, four-seater tourer.

Twin spares are carried in a well at the rear. Note huge cap on the 27-gallon gas tank.

(Left) Detail of the steering knuckle and brake-drum assembly. (Right) Dash and cockpit of the Mercedes. Controls to the four-speed gearbox were now located centrally, to allow for left- or right-hand drive. (Photo by Saul)

The S series is notable for its lowered frame, giving better stability at high speed. The SSK models were on a shortened wheelbase and attained still higher speeds. The ultimate expression of the Porsche design was the dozen or so SSKL models (the L for *leicht,* or light), which were factory racing-team specials. The engine was fitted with a high-lift camshaft, high-compression pistons, and the granddaddy of all *Kompressors,* the "Elephant" blower. A heavily stiffened crankshaft was necessary to handle the 300-plus horsepower produced. The frame was turned into a veritable Swiss cheese, with huge holes cut to reduce weight. The perforations must have weakened the car as well, but few drivers outside the "works" team ever drove these cars, so little concern was voiced. The big blower put air into the carburetor at 12 pounds per square inch, and 15 seconds was the recommended limit of each dramatic application.

The SS illustrated was raced at LeMans in 1929 by no less a figure than Sir Malcolm Campbell; he placed tenth. The following year at the big Tourist Trophy race in Ireland, the British speed king had words with the German team leader, Caracciola. He objected to the Mercedes team entry being fitted with the potent "Elephant" blower when it was not available to the public. As all entries were required to be "stock," his objections were upheld, and presumably, the blower was removed. But the great German driver continued to win, taking the Irish Grand Prix and exceeding 90 mph on one lap.

Actual top speeds of the various models is a controversial subject. Private owners of all models, regardless of coachwork, were attaining 100 mph regularly. The car in racing form, with the open two-seater or close-coupled four-passenger body, could reach speeds up to 118 mph, depending on axle ratio and compression ratio in use. One Swiss-cheese SSKL, with a special streamlined body, was driven on the Avus circuit in Berlin by Von Brauchitsch at 156 mph in 1931.

The Valkyrie shriek of the supercharger being cut in must have had an interesting psychological effect on competing drivers. From a harrowing drive in a Mercedes 540 K, I can attest to its ability to spread alarm throughout the countryside. With their enormous power and demanding brakes, these cars were not for the Sunday sports-car buff. They are without doubt the most sought after of the classic European record-breakers of the twenties. Those lucky few who own a Mercedes-Benz of the Porsche era would consider it reckless indeed to drive the car today as it was built to be driven. Perhaps that is good insurance that future generations will be able to examine such examples as the one here illustrated, now preserved in the Motor Museum at Ellenville, New York.

By 1928, displacement had been increased to over 7 liters; output was normally 170 horsepower, and 225 with the supercharger engaged. The blower is mounted vertically on the crankcase, ahead of the block. (Photo by Saul)

Exhaust side of the Porsche-designed six. (Photo by Saul)

Horizontal hood louvers add to the impression of length on the Jordan factory-bodied phaeton. (Photography by permission of the Frederick C. Crawford Auto-Aviation Museum, Western Reserve Historical Society, Cleveland, Ohio.)

1929 JORDAN PHAETON MODEL G

THE JORDAN is best remembered for inspiring the purple prose that brought romance to automotive advertising. Before President Ned Jordan wrote his own glowing copy, auto ads were steeped in learned discussions of Timken axles, vanadium steel, double dropped frames, and the like. Jordan was the first to realize that to many people, driving was an experience of strong emotional involvement. Up to that time copy writers had been writing ads as if to woo the engineering profession exclusively.

Ned Jordan reached out for the late-hour fantasies of the man resting from the practical worries and cares of the real world and gave him escape—if only he owned a Jordan. The siren called thus: "Somewhere far beyond the place where men and motors race through canyons of the town—there lies the Port of Missing Men. It may be in the valley of our dreams of youth, or on the heights of future happy days. Go there in November when the logs are blazing in the grate, go there in a Jordan Playboy if you love the spirit of youth. Escape the drab of dull winter's coming—leave the roar of city streets and spend an hour in Eldorado."

While few car makers had directed their advertising copy to women since the demise of electrics, Jordan called to every starry-eyed young woman in the country with this now immortal appeal: "Somewhere west of Laramie there's a bronco-busting, steer-roping gal who knows what I'm talking about. She can tell what a sassy pony, that's a cross between greased lightning and the place where it hits, can do with 1100 pounds of steel and action when he's going high, wide, and handsome ... the Playboy was built for her."

Behind all this beguiling language there was a car of considerable merit. From the early days in Cleveland, Edward S. Jordan built his cars of the best available components. Continental provided Jordan with engines from the firm's first 1916 models to the last straight eight in 1931. The car had a consistently stylish appearance. In describing their aluminum-bodied "Silhouette Sedan," Jordan modestly claimed that the car was three years ahead of the times.

The five-liter, six-cylinder engine powered all models until the Continental straight eight was introduced in 1925. Production in 1926 topped 10,000 units,

This view shows rear cowl in place with doors open. Dual cowl must be raised to allow passengers to enter, then lowered in place.

The Jordan front end is distinguished by clean lines rather than unique design.

Detail shows attractive fittings of the dual sidemounts.

which was to be Jordan's high-water mark. With all the luxury cars being offered with expensive custom bodies, Jordan offered a luxury six called the "Little Custom." Surprisingly, it had little appeal and few were sold. The company tried to span the medium-to-luxury price range, which had seldom worked well for other car builders. In their last years Jordan offered cars from $1295 to $5000.

The autos' outstanding features were strength without weight, pleasing lines, and dependable if not daring engineering. The romantic appeal of their ads usually ended with a practical note—a reminder that Jordans were the lightest cars for their wheelbase made in America, and that they held a national economy record of 24 miles per gallon.

The stylish phaeton illustrated, a fine example of the classic lines of the factory-made bodies, is somewhat reminiscent of the Auburn of the period. The car is on a long 125-inch wheelbase and the eight-cylinder Continental engine displaces 268 cubic inches. The fine restoration was undertaken by the Lester Tire Company in 1970, and the car is on display at the Frederick C. Crawford Auto-Aviation Museum in Cleveland, Ohio.

Jordan launched their most ambitious model in the ill-fated year of 1930. Designated the Speedway Eight, the big Continental engine was rated at 114 horsepower and mated to a four-speed transmission. Despite attractive coach-work, it found few buyers; for the same price one could purchase a Packard Model 734 boattail speedster. Within a year the Cleveland company ceased production and joined Kissel, Erskine, Peerless, Essex, Viking, and Ruxton in that graveyard where tottering auto firms went to die. It is sobering to think that these makes, some whose history began in the very infancy of the industry, all collapsed within a period of twenty-four months.

Immaculate restoration of the Continental straight eight. The 268-cubic-inch engine develops 90 horsepower for a cruising speed of 65 mph.

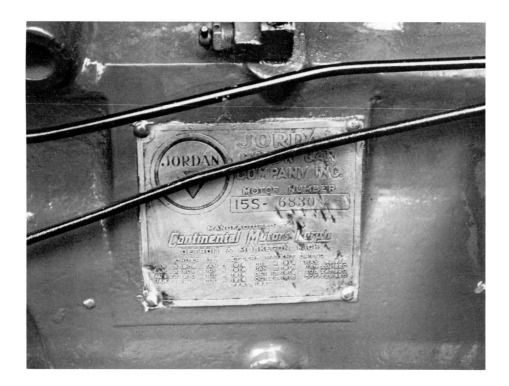

Engine plate of the Jordan.

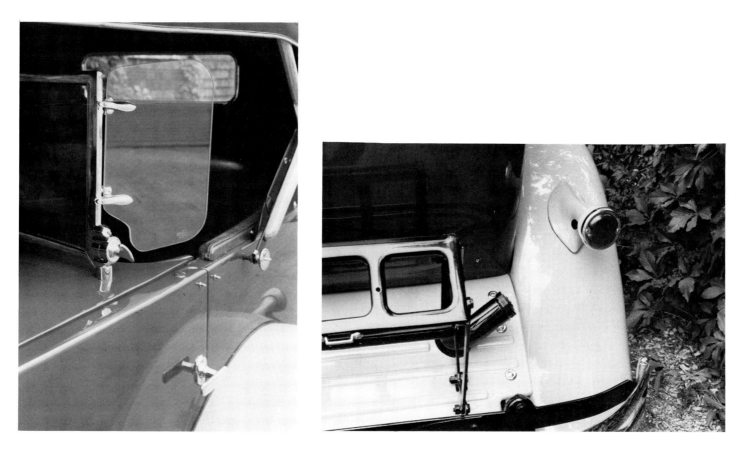

(Left) Detail of rear folding windscreen and windwing. (Right) Trunk rack and taillight detail of the Jordan phaeton.

The Playboy — *by Jordan*

The Playboy Roadster as offered in 1922.

Of some seven hundred 4½-liter Bentleys made, only fifty or so were equipped with the Amherst Villiers Supercharger.

1930 BENTLEY
4½-LITER TOURER
Body by Vanden Plas

ALTHOUGH true Bentleys were built only from 1921 to 1931, the name Bentley has remained on various luxury cars for the past four decades. in the past twenty years, the name and a special grille have served only to mask the identity of a production Rolls-Royce for those who wanted that car in a more anonymous form. To the collector, the name Bentley recalls a brilliant but modest Englishman, whose great, green, cycle-fendered brutes bore the Union Jack to victory over the world's best racing cars on the fiercely competitive tracks of the twenties.

Despite such great achievements on road and track, the company never really prospered to the point of financial security. Most astonishing of all, when the man who virtually alone brought England victory after victory in international road-racing competition faced economic collapse, the British government remained indifferent. What some countries would have regarded as a national treasure was viewed by London officialdom as an ungainly and noisy motor car, in which a band of rather reckless amateurs slashed about the European countryside. Many of the drivers were essentially part-time, amateur sportsmen, who on occasion entered their personal Bentleys because the factory could not afford an official entry! This particular breed of competitor was distinctively English, cultivating the casual, understated approach to road racing. Their urbane manner at first deceived the professional "works" teams of France and Germany, who soon found out that it cloaked a savage determination to win. The "Bentley Boys" were of the same stamp as the men who would in a few years take their yachts to lift an army from the Dunkirk beaches, and who would exchange their bucket seats for Spitfire cockpits with equal aplomb and success.

Young W. O. Bentley was born at just the right time for the rapid development of his considerable engineering gifts. When he was sixteen, just a year after the Wright Brothers first flew at Kitty Hawk, he was apprenticed to the

The body most commonly used on the 130-inch chassis is this stark Vanden Plas four-seater open tourer.

engineering works of the Great Northern Railway Company. The technology of the locomotive was well advanced in those years and the railway shop was the cradle of learning for many future automotive greats. After completing his apprenticeship in 1910, Bentley supervised the maintenance of a fleet of London cabs for two years.

"W.O." and his brother teamed up to sell motorcars in 1912, marketing the imported French D.F.P. in their Hanover Street showrooms. It was here that the Bentley urge to improve, to change, and to excel came to the fore. Intrigued by the rugged 15-horsepower four-cylinder engine that powered the French car, Bentley made extensive modifications and succeeded in radically improving the car's performance. The Bentley magic transformed the sedate 2-liter into a sports car that took several wins at Brooklands.

By the time war broke out in 1914, Bentley was well known in engineering circles. The Bentley piston for aircraft engines was used in several makes, and it might surprise some auto buffs to know that later production of his great car engines never approached the staggering total of 30,000 Bentley Rotary Aero engines that were built in the war years.

Immediately after the armistice, "W.O." shook off the restrictions of military service, which had restrained his impatient urge to experiment, and with some friends founded Bentley Motors. The goal: a high-speed, comfortable, and perfect-handling sports tourer.

Although the famed 3-liter that resulted was shown in 1919, it was 1921 before the firm's threadbare financing allowed production to begin. This first Bentley engine to win fame on the track featured four cylinders, a head and block cast in one piece, four valves per cylinder, and a single overhead camshaft.

Realizing that the road to fame was not commercial advertising but victory at the track, Bentley entered their 3-liters in the important Tourist Trophy Race held in 1922 on the Isle of Man. The three-car team placed second, fourth, and fifth, stirring instant speculation and discussion of Bentley cars. The well-financed factory teams of France and Germany were forced to take notice of the Bentley threat when a private entry driven by John Duff won the Le Mans in 1924.

Bentley production was never high, and the entire run of the 3-liter series between 1921 and 1927 was fewer than 1700 vehicles. Most of these were fitted with the classic open tourer body, either two- or four-seater, depending on the wheelbase and the buyer's desire. "W.O." had not lost sight of his original goal, however, and next produced the Big Six, which was practically a sports-type limousine, having ample chassis for any type of custom body and 85-mph performance. The 6½-liter six was a superb engine, displacing over 400 cubic inches with a compression ratio of 4.4 to 1. With many refinements to ensure

(Above) The overhead camshaft four-cylinder Bentley engine displaced over 400 cubic inches. (Below) Cockpit of the Bentley is strictly utilitarian. Note speedometer is calibrated to 130 mph.

almost silent operation while turning at a peak of 3500 rpm, the Big Six (in chassis alone) cost over $7000.

In 1927 the aging 3-liter was replaced with the Bentley of now legendary fame, the 4½-liter. This machine mated the 269-cubic-inch four-cylinder to a close-ratio four-speed transmission and a chassis capable of absorbing the savage pounding of the worst roads in the world.

This Bentley was the star of perhaps the most-talked-of race in road competition, the 1927 Le Mans. The story has been told at length elsewhere, but the drama of the White House Corner crash is the stuff that legends are truly made of. In the gloom of night, six cars were involved in a mass pile-up at a French village corner. One of three Bentleys extricated itself from the wreckage, and though "totaled" by today's standards, drove on into the rain-whipped night, thirty miles behind the leader, a French Aries. Driven alternately by Sammy Davis and Dr. J. D. Benjafield, this rolling wreck, crippled by a twisted axle, defective steering, mangled fenders, faulty brakes, and missing two of its three road lights, went on to win.

The car illustrated is of this breed, a doughty 4½-liter still capable of threading the hairpin mountain curves of New York's Catskills at high speed as though glued to the road. The impressive supercharger, which boosts its performance remarkably, was never approved by W. O. Bentley himself. Its installation reduced the reliability of the car, and it is significant that "blown" 4½-liters never won a major race.

Most of the 4½-liters carried bodies similar to the Vanden Plas coachwork shown here. One of the car's few annoying characteristics is that it overheats at idle or low speed; it is not equipped with a fan, so our drive out of town to demonstrate the car's remarkable handling was accompanied by wreaths of steam pouring from the radiator cap. Once at speed, this problem disappears.

In 1931, just before the financial strain was to prove fatal, Bentley achieved his long-sought dream and finally built a high-speed road car combining the ultimate in comfort and excellent handling. The 8-liter model had a production run of scarcely a hundred cars, with varied and exotic bodies. A twenty-year-old specimen that was run, under official rules on a European autobahn in 1950, broke numerous world records. These stock-production 8-liters are still capable today of speeds in excess of 140 mph.

The greatest tribute that can be paid to the Bentleys is that despite their rapidly increasing value as museum pieces, they are still being enthusiastically raced by many of their devoted owners today.

(Left) Vanden Plas body plate. (Below) The enormous "blower" is carried ahead of the carburetor and barely fits within the frame rails.

(Above) Four-wheel brakes on the 4½-liter model were highly effective, stopping the car in 56 feet from 40 mph. (Right) Hefty ignition and throttle controls are featured on the Bentley steering wheel.

*(Above) Cycle fenders leave much
of running gear exposed. (Left)
Bentley crest and quick-fill radiator
cap top the lofty radiator.*

Rear view features enormous gas tank and huge brake drums.

1930 RUXTON ROADSTER

IN THEORY, a great automobile should spring from a team of experts. Engineering of both the power train and the chassis should be of the highest order. Unlimited funds and the most advanced shop with plenty of highly skilled craftsmen favor the flowering of automotive genius. In harmony with such a staff, a brilliant styling team would ensure the perfect blend of engineering, riding comfort, and beautiful design. To these assets should be added the tranquility of a generous development schedule.

Given these rules, it is all the more incredible that a handful of talented people, working in the all-time corporate chaos attending the stock-market crash of 1929, did produce a superlative, radically advanced new motorcar.

The records identify the Ruxton as the product of New Era Motors, Inc. Banish the picture of a humming plant with orderly executive offices overlooking busy production lines; no such Ruxton factory ever existed. This remarkable car was designed by veteran Budd engineer William Muller, but it was actually manufactured in fits and starts, involving at least eight auto companies, almost all of them in their death throes.

The decisions and counterdecisions began in 1928, when Archie M. Andrews, a Hupp director, saw the hand-built prototype of the front-wheel-drive auto that Muller had built in the Budd body shop. Andrews was also on the board of the Budd Company, and his proposal to promote the new car was reluctantly agreed to. The first decision to fall apart was Andrews' plan to build the new car in the Hupp plant. That company had a fast-selling car at the moment and didn't care to yield floor space to an untried front-drive newcomer.

While engineer Muller chased all over, preparing tooling for components of the production sedan, the search went on for a home plant. Gardner and Marmon were both considered, and each announced at different times that they would build the new Ruxton. Even naming the car wasn't routine. Prominent Wall Streeter William V. Ruxton, none too happy that his name was being used, went to court to disassociate himself from the company.

While the car's technical problems were being ironed out, it was finally determined that the two companies comprising New Era Motors would be Kissel and Moon. The Moon plant in St. Louis, Missouri, built the chassis, with Budd

(Opposite) Distinctive headlights and flaring fenders mark the front end of the Ruxton.

Low silhouette, long hood, and lack of running boards set the Ruxton immediately apart.

Louvered side panels can be removed for easier access to the Continental straight eight. Dual sidemounts were standard equipment on all models.

The Ruxton is deceptively long, and the rumble seat is unusually spacious.

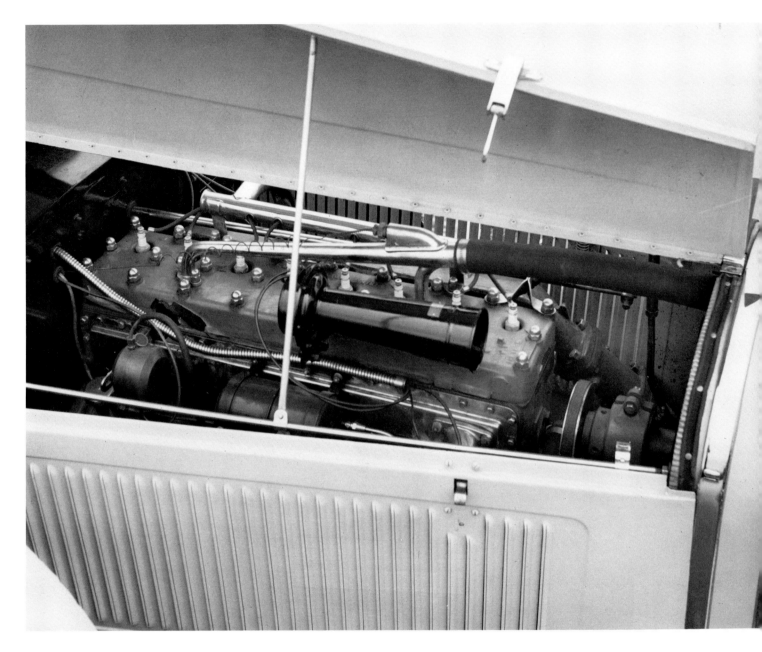

The standard Continental engine was successfully turned around by engineer Muller to power the front-drive car.

Part of the Ruxton's visual appeal is in its 19-inch Budd disc wheels and the special striping that highlights the lines of the body.

making sedan bodies and the Raulang Company of Cleveland making the production roadster body. When it finally seemed that volume production could seriously begin (a substantial number of orders were in by June of 1930), one of the keystones of the shaky structure, Kissel, folded. George Kissel apparently preferred receivership to yielding control of his failing company to Andrews. Unfortunately, all final drive units were being built in the Kissel plant, and closing down those production lines effectively shut down the Moon plant as well. Moon followed Kissel, and New Era followed both into bankruptcy shortly thereafter.

The tangle of corporate machinations and lawsuits that overshadowed the all-too-brief life of the Ruxton should not obscure the quality of the car itself. In many ways it was more successful in its engineering concept than its rival, the L-29 Cord. The design of the roadster and sedan bodies flowed from the low-chassis front-drive concept, and was easily a decade ahead of its time.

Motor Magazine at the time heralded the Ruxton as "America's first front-drive car," though the Cord actually made it to the salesroom first. Much was made of having 42 inches of headroom in a car that stood 60 inches high yet cleared the road by a full 10 inches.

The layout of the power train is unusual; the 100-horsepower straight-eight Continental engine is reversed, with the bell housing up front. The clutch is forward of the engine, and ahead of the clutch is a Muller-designed 3-speed transmission, with the differential housing directly attached to it. The Kissel-built final drive is divided by the differential, with first and reverse forward, and second and high gears to the rear. The gearshift control to this far-from-the-driver gearbox is a handle that protrudes horizontally from under the dash.

The chassis is of rugged construction; the frame rails are 6½ inches deep with 2-inch-wide flanges. No less than seven cross members give the chassis unusual strength and provide mounting foundations for the seats. Lockheed hydraulic brakes on all four wheels are employed. Steering is a worm-and-roller

Detail of the stoplight unit.

Designed according to an elaborate optical theory, Woodlites' lighting output is questionable, though its beauty is not.

type made by Gemmer. The exotically shaped "Woodlites" were not considered to provide adequate lighting by several state motor vehicle departments at the time, but it must be admitted that they add enormously to the style of the car.

The Ruxton was not around long enough as a production car to be road tested and evaluated against its 1930 competitors. Bill Muller loaned his short-wheelbase prototype (equipped with a supercharger) to several ranking drivers at the Indy 500, and they turned 105 mph in it with ease. So few exist today, it seems unlikely that a Ruxton owner could be found to test the car to its limit.

The roadster illustrated is one of approximately 250 assembled at the Kissel plant in Hartford, Wisconsin, with the standard Raulang body. Andrew Adler acquired the car from the noted Cameron Peck collection. It had been well maintained since its original purchase by a lady driver in Connecticut. New leather, a new top, and paint have brought the machine to a high point winning status.

Few automobiles have achieved the overall high level of daring design and successful technical execution of the Ruxton. Surely no other accomplished it within a production lifespan of just six months.

In keeping with the emphasis on low-line styling, the Ruxton emblem is recessed in the grille.

(Above) Elegant driver's compartment features horizontally mounted gearshift lever and flat floor. (Right) All instruments are grouped in one center panel.

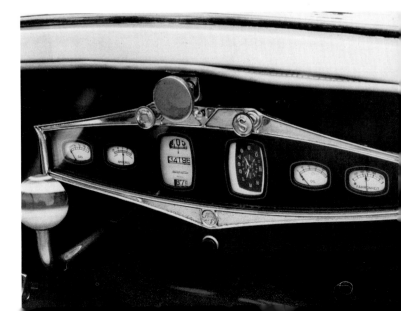

Front view of the V-16 convertible coupe.

1932 MARMON V-16 CONVERTIBLE COUPE

MARMON shared with Studebaker the distinction of having existed, as a company, before the Civil War. While Studebaker was building wagons, the firm of Nordyke and Marmon was making milling machinery. Howard Marmon, who was to direct the family firm into the automobile business, was born in 1876. With his older brother, Walter, he got a thorough practical grounding in manufacturing skills in their milling-machinery plant. Howard was naturally inclined toward things mechanical, which led him to take an engineering degree just in time for the automobile boom that swept the country at the turn of the century.

After four years of tinkering in his spare hours, Howard wheeled his first hand-built vehicle out to the streets of Indianapolis. The V twin-cylinder engine was novel in that lubrication was pressure-fed to the engine bearings by means of a drilled crankshaft. As a test bed for Marmon's ideas on suspension, engine design, and other novel features, the car was a success. It led almost immediately to a V-4 design that was so refined and reliable for the time (1904) that the firm agreed to make replicas for six customers who requested a "Marmon."

Over the next five years Marmon decided that he could not succeed with a car based on the air-cooled engine. A last abortive attempt was made to market an expensive V-8, but it received a chilly reception, and the big, aluminum-bodied $5000 Model 37 was never put in production.

Once the decision was made to settle for a water-cooled engine, everything seemed to go right for the fledgling auto division of Nordyke and Marmon. The new Model 32 took first place in one of the early races held at the brand-new Indianapolis speedway in 1909. With that, Howard Marmon reversed his position (he had always said racing "specials" were irrelevant to the production cars that customers drove), and entered his new four-cylinder in every event in sight. Within two years, Marmons won 35 firsts, 30 seconds, and 20 thirds, which added up to placing in the top three slots 85 times out of 113 races entered. The landmark victory that really counted was Ray Harroun crossing the finish line first at the inaugural Indy 500 in 1911. His Marmon "Wasp" was hardly a production car, but its 75 mph average and the reliable Marmon engineering finally made the factory car one to reckon with. Orders flowed in, and the Model 32 continued in production for seven years.

The best known Marmon, other than the illustrious V-16, followed in 1915. The Model 34 was very advanced for its time; it featured a pushrod-operated overhead-valve six-cylinder engine with an aluminum crankcase. It developed about 75 horsepower at 2450 rpm and displaced 340 cubic inches. Again Howard Marmon used aluminum for almost the entire body. The early start that the new and wondrous metal got in the automotive field must be credited largely to this far-sighted engineer. Only Pierce Arrow ever attempted the large aluminum body castings that were now routine at Marmon. As the Model 34 weighed only slightly over 3000 pounds, the big six gave it sparkling performance with a top speed of 70 mph. In 1916, the new car set a coast-to-coast speed record via the new Lincoln Highway. The Marmon lopped 41 hours off the recent record set by "Cannonball" Baker in a Cadillac V-8.

Although the Model 34 had bested Cadillac in the field, the salesroom story was something different: Marmon was still struggling to produce more than 1000 cars a year, while the smoothly running Cadillac organization was building and selling some 15,000 autos yearly. Preoccupation with car design and less interest in the art of volume production was Marmon's great problem until the end.

For today's collector, the most desirable of all Model 34s is the speedster, introduced in 1920. What is universally referred to now as boattail styling, Marmon called "turtleback" design. Although it seems a poor choice of word to associate with speed, the car itself was fast. With its aluminum body, weight was held to less than 3500 pounds. Top speed was over 80 mph. On its long wheelbase of 136 inches, the clean-lined machine brought people into the showrooms; unfortunately, the price tag of $5300 sent most of them quickly out again. Four-wheel brakes became an option in 1923, and despite drastic price reductions to $2985 in 1924, the speedster model was a disappointing seller.

In the years between the Model 34 and the V-16 swan song, the company was reorganized and management changed several times. The correct decision to drop sixes and build only eights was made, and just in time. Unfortunately, Marmon found that some of the prestige of a fine name is lost when it is placed on a low-priced car. The Little Marmon was introduced in 1927 to sell for under $2000, and the Roosevelt was offered in 1929 at less than $1000. Both were good cars, and the Roosevelt a remarkable value, but they did not prepare the public for a new $5500 luxury auto. The big eights, at $3000 to $4500, sold very well, with banner sales of 22,000 in 1929.

The little Roosevelt proved that Marmon reliability was built into even the cheapest model. In June of 1929, a team of AAA officials selected a Roosevelt sedan at random from the production line and took it to the Indianapolis

Elegant and unadorned Marmon V-16 scorned headlight crossbar and front-mounted trumpet horns.

Despite a wheelbase of 145 inches, overall length is 216 inches. Six-ply tires are 7.00 by 18.

Speedway for an economy run demonstration. By switching drivers and refueling from a moving "mother" car, the Roosevelt was able to drive continuously. In 440 hours it covered 13,457 miles at a steady 30 mph, non stop.

In 1931 Marmon introduced the V-16, the result of six years of development. The car failed to sell well for two obvious reasons: the depression, which wiped out the luxury-car-buying class almost en masse, and the fact that over 2000 turbine-smooth Cadillac V-16s were already on the highway. The Marmon V-16 was, however, probably the most advanced car of the period in its combination of power, smoothness, and body styling. The 1930 line of Cadillacs, with their beautifully built Fleetwood bodies, showed only the most minute changes from the lines of 1928; the Marmon V-16 sedan would still look current in 1935.

The Marmon masterpiece could attain a speed of 105 mph, despite a weight of 5300 pounds. Packard, Pierce, Auburn, and Cadillac might have their V-12s and V-16s but only the Marmon developed 200 horsepower. Although the Duesenberg eight-cylinder was much more powerful, the custom-styled Marmon cost $3000 less than the bare "Duesy" chassis alone. The aluminum engine that Marmon designed weighed only 930 pounds, roughly 400 pounds less than if iron and steel had been used.

The engine displaced 490 cubic inches, used overhead valves, and was capable of moving the heavy sedan from a standing start to a mile-a-minute speed in just 14 seconds. The chassis was conventional but every bit up to the engine. On a 145-inch wheelbase, the suspension was by large semielliptic springs front and rear. Braking was mechanical on all front wheels with 16-inch drums. Power brakes were standard, and the big car could be stopped as efficiently as the smaller Marmons.

The V-16 was admired, and undoubtedly the smooth styling of the body, designed by famed Walter Dorwin Teague and built by Le Baron, would have helped sales in normal times. These were not normal times, however, and total sales for the three years that the V-16 was offered were a dismal 390 machines. The company was reorganized after receivership in 1931 as the still thriving Marmon-Herrington Company.

The convertible coupe shown was located in Colorado. Its condition was poor, but the aluminum body was sound. Because Marmon pioneered the extensive use of aluminum, the V-16 bodies are usually thought to be all aluminum. The body shell, fenders, and doors of the sedan are steel, however. A full restoration was performed on this convertible, and the car cruises today, as the press noted in 1931, "exceedingly smooth with very light controls."

This specimen is one of seven known examples of the convertible coupe body style. Perhaps in the gloomy corner of an estate garage somewhere, another V-16 convertible awaits discovery. It is not entirely impossible, as the records show that Le Baron built forty-four of this glamorous model.

The V-16 engine is a 45-degree-angle V-type, and the aluminum alloy block is a one-piece casting. Steel cylinder liners were used to lengthen the engine life. Displacement is 490.8 with a compression ratio of 6.0.

(Above) Detail of rumble seat and trunk rack. (Below) Large instruments are located at eye level on the polished dash. Airplane-type controls for choke, throttle, spark, and carburetor heat protrude just below.

MARMON *custom-built* motor cars

with bodies by Locke

MARMON
SIXTEEN

The Marmon Sixteen is the modern automobile. Its beaut,

and appointment is the beauty of the simplicity and effic

today. Its 200-horsepower engine is an achievement of g

portance. Its mechanical excellence has been proved by fo

of painstaking development. Both in action and appearance t

mon Sixteen redefines the motor car in terms of the present. Wh

145 inches. Prices under $5000. Marmon Motor Car Co., Indic

(Left) Marmon offered their big eight, series 75, with custom bodies by Locke, Le Baron, and others in this 1927 advertisement. (Right) For once, a car ad actually understates the case. The V-16 engine earned Howard Marmon the coveted Society of Automotive Engineers medal for 1931.

Detail of door.

Stamina as well as beauty was a quality of the V-16 Marmon. A stock model sedan won the Steven trophy in 1931 with an average speed of 76 mph during the 24-hour test.

Distinctive Duesenberg front end features huge headlights and bow-shaped bumper.

1932 DUESENBERG J SPEEDSTER
Body by Murphy

THE "J" Duesenberg is widely accepted as the finest automobile ever designed and built by an American firm; it is only because of the admirers of the V-16 series Marmon and Cadillac that we say "widely accepted," rather than "universally accepted."

The Model J was the result of the longest gestation period of any great car. Fred Duesenberg, the engineer, and his brother, August, the planner and manager, formed a brilliant team.

Starting with farm implements in 1894, moving on to racing bicycles in 1897, and finally to automobiles in 1904, Fred Duesenberg continually grew as an engineer. Their first automotive company was named for its backer, and the two-cylinder Mason was Fred's first car. In the years just before the European war broke out, the Duesenberg brothers and a bright young mechanic-driver named Eddie Rickenbacker built many racing variants of the Mason and devoted most of their time to the track.

Duesenberg Motors was formed in 1913, and until the appearance of their first production car in 1921, the brothers built marine engines and complete racing cars. The best-known Duesenberg design of this period was the horizontal-valve engine, later made by Rochester Motors and used in Roamer, Meteor, and other quality cars.

In 1921 a Duesenberg straight-eight won the French Grand Prix, the first American car to win that event. It was an appropriate time to offer the public a production luxury car bearing the Duesenberg name. A new organization had been formed in Indianapolis the year before, named the Duesenberg Automobile & Motors Corporation. Their model A was the first production car made in America to offer a straight-eight engine and four-wheel hydraulic brakes. The 260-cubic-inch motor was rated at 100 horsepower. Despite its large size, the open tourer weighed only 3100 pounds. Some 500 of the Model A series were built through 1927.

Probably the largest boattail speedster built, the Murphy body is on the 142½-inch Duesenberg chassis.

In 1926, E. L. Cord entered the picture, and it was his money, ideas, and enthusiasm that led to the capstone of the Duesenberg brothers' achievements, the legendary Model J. Cord had just become president of Auburn in February of 1926; in a rapid series of moves, he acquired the Duesenberg Company and controlling interest in Lycoming Motors and the Limousine Body Company. Fred Duesenberg was retained as engineering vice-president and was immediately asked to design the ultimate luxury car. Cord intended to lure the banker-class clientele away from those magical names of Rolls, Mercedes, Isotta, and Hispano-Suiza with an all-American car that would outclass all foreign competition.

Shown in 1928, the first J models were available in April of 1929. No aspect of a fine car was overlooked; the new chassis was available for custom coachwork by fourteen prestige body builders. In addition, young Gordon Buehrig, later to style the incomparable 810 Cord, headed up a factory design team. Because the factory kept rigid control of the front-end design of the car, all custom-bodied Js were instantly recognizable as Duesenbergs. The chassis was available only with standard grille, headlamps, bumpers, hood, fenders, and even running boards in place. The custom body firms accepted this without complaint, such was the prestige and cachet of the Duesenberg name.

Beneath the glittering body, the chassis and engine teamed to create a production passenger car that could compete with most pure competition racers in the world.

The straight eight displaces 420 cubic inches, with a bore and stroke of 3¾ by 4¾ inches. At 4200 rpm it develops 265 horsepower, fantastic for the time. Its racing ancestry is evident in the four valves per cylinder actuated by double overhead silent chain-driven camshafts. The cylinder block and the upper half of the crankcase is cast in one rigid piece, and the crankshaft is fitted with a mercury vibration dampener. Much aluminum was used to save weight, and the cooling system was extremely efficient for continuous high speed touring.

Instrumentation to supervise this superb engine was complete down to warning lights indicating the need for oil change, battery inspection, and refueling, and included a 5000-rpm tachometer and a speedometer calibrated to 150 mph.

In terms of performance, the car was unique. With a typical curb weight of 5000 to 7000 pounds, the Duesenberg was capable of doing 90 mph in second gear and 119 in high. The supercharged version, the SJ could attain 100 mph from a standing start in just 20 seconds.

The Model J shown is one of five boattailed speedsters built by Murphy, whose firm built fifty-five roadster bodies as well. Murphy delivered all five boattails to the factory in 1929. Two were completed for the 1930 auto shows, and two others were completed soon after and sold.

This Duesenberg has an interesting history, having passed through the hands

The ultimate Duesenberg engine: 420 cubic inches, 265 horsepower, compression 5.2 to 1.

Detail showing external exhausts on right side of the straight-eight Duesenberg engine.

of at least six owners. It was completed and sold in early 1932 to Cliff Durant, son of General Motors' W. C. Durant. Present owner Don Carr acquired the car in 1951 from a Cleveland man. The car had been much altered, and it was a rather tired and ratty specimen. The headlights were from a 1937 or 1938 Buick, the bumpers were postwar Detroit products, the door handles and taillights were nonoriginal. Cheap discs had been fitted over the original chromed wire wheels. Two-inch lowering blocks were under the rear springs, and one running board was a length of wooden planking.

Several years of hunting produced the needed original equipment, and much work on the engine has brought it back to its original performance. The odometer indicated 49,870 miles at the time of purchase in 1952. The condition of the car leads Mr. Carr to believe it had gone "around the clock" once before. If that is the case, the 100,000 miles its present owner has put on the car make it a quarter-of-a-million-mile Duesy!

Motor numbers for the series were started at J-101; this engine plate reads J-476. The chassis is No. 2485, and the Murphy body is No. 906. To the Duesenberg detective these numbers are significant, because many cars were completed (bodied) long after the chassis was built. Fewer than five hundred Js were built, including some thirty-eight supercharged SJ's. Most were on the short (142½ inch) wheelbase. Original cost was very high, the chassis of the J running $8500 and the SJ, $11,750. Despite legends of $100,000 cars, few Duesenbergs cost more than $20,000, even with the most expensive coachwork. Consider, however, that the superb Marmon V-16 was $5000 complete, and the Cadillac Fleetwood Imperials ran under $7000.

In 1932 Fred Duesenberg, then fifty-five, was killed when his SJ left a rain-slicked mountain road in Pennsylvania. August carried on until the market evaporated in 1937 and attempted one unsuccessful revival of the make in 1947. He was seventy-five when he died in 1955.

Mr. Carr's speedster is likely the last Duesy to be used and enjoyed as a normal motorcar. In everyday driving, the owner has made many long trips

Interior of the Murphy speedster is restored for "go" rather than show.

(Above) Front end showing external pipes on right side of hood. (Right) Taillight detail shows flare of boattail design.

*Disappearing top folded into storage compart-
ment with panel in open position.*

with the only difficulty an occasional explanation to a state trooper concerning the rather audible muffler cut-out. With the value of this gem rising rapidly and parts becoming scarce, even a minor low-speed collision could become a disaster.

It is a tribute to the Duesenberg that during the scrap drives and gas rationing of World War II, when so many classics went to the boneyard, almost 300 of the 480 J's made were preserved. Beautifully restored and regularly shown, many of these cars represent the last, and finest, spine-tingling trumpet call of the classic era.

Rumble seat open and top stored.

Profile of clean-lined speedster with top down.

Skirting on front fenders is not original, but result of customizing by an earlier owner. Chrome covers on side-mounted spares were provided by factory, and these are still being sought by the owner.

Styling flair is built into the Duesenberg by grille and hood design. Regardless of what custom body was fitted, each J retained its instantly recognizable Duesenberg identity.

1937 CORD S/C 812
SPORTSMAN

IN THE early thirties, E. L. Cord was trying valiantly to bring order for his auto empire out of chaos created largely by the depression. He had taken the almost moribund Auburn Company, and with bold styling paired with the Lycoming engine he controlled, had created an exciting line of cars. He had grasped that Fred and August Duesenberg were capable of building the finest car in America, and with his support they had done just that, with the incomparable J Duesenberg.

Cord realized that to compete with the Detroit giants, his cars must be bold, innovative, and different. Hence the effort to market a successful front-drive car. In 1930, inspired by the Harry Miller racing cars, he launched the L-29. This was a conventional luxury car in general appearance, except for its unusual low-swept lines. Under the hood was a straight-eight Lycoming engine, reversed, as in the Ruxton. But the double universal joints on each front axle half absorbed a beating, since the braking torque was transferred to the front wheels directly through these delicate universals. Mounting the brakes on the wheels instead of inboard might have remedied this weakness.

It was unfortunate that Cord's ingenious engineering hadn't solved all the problems inherent in the straight-eight L-29, because the car was a remarkable value in every other way. It cost only $3000, but easily ranked with the senior Packards and Cadillacs in materials, features, and finish. Lockheed four-wheel hydraulic brakes and the expensive Bijur automatic chassis lube system were standard, as were sporty wire wheels with knock-off hubs. The long wheelbase of 137½ inches made for attractive looks and was rather necessary to pack all that train of front-drive machinery under the nearly six-foot-long hood. The differential was carried so far forward that it was incorporated in the grille and bumper arrangement as an esthetic part of the front-end design.

Rather tricky to drive, particularly in hilly country, the Cord acquired a reputation for rapid front-end wear and the need for frequent maintenance. Only 4429 were sold in the three years that Auburn dealers offered the car. Meanwhile the Auburn itself was selling well, and as it became apparent that the Duesenberg market was rapidly disappearing, Erret Cord decided to try

(Opposite) Striking front end of the 1937 Cord, possibly the most original and timeless automobile design ever produced in the United States.

again in the middle price range with another front-drive model. By the mid-thirties engineering had advanced to make a front-drive car more reliable. The big headache of the L-29, the pesky double universals, were replaced by a single, constant-velocity unit. Independent suspension was also a welcome improvement. The new Lycoming V-8 was much better suited to forward-drive weight distribution than was the old straight-eight used in the L-29.

The new car was designed by Gordon Buehrig. In terms of industrial design, few American cars have earned the accolades that the Cord 810 and 812 have. Each new generation of car buffs that sees it for the first time is fascinated by its bold and original beauty. It might be called America's Bugatti, in that it is the work of one inspired man, borrowing so little from what went before. The design went back to 1933, when Buehrig was assigned to style a medium-priced car to carry the Duesenberg name. Even then Cord realized that the depressed economy dictated that a new car should cost under $3000 if it were to have any chance of success. Unfortunately, that project was shelved, and Buehrig was sent over to facelift the Auburn line in 1934. He was recalled in mid-1935 and asked to complete the baby Duesenberg as a front-drive Cord in time for the November deadline of the New York auto show.

In a herculean effort, the brilliant engineering and factory staff complied with the stringent show requirements and hand-built the necessary one hundred cars. Had the company elected to postpone the new Cord until the following year and methodically worked out the bugs in the meantime, perhaps the make would still be with us. Instead, the new car was acclaimed, ordered in delightful numbers, and then could not be delivered because of delays in manufacturing the transmission. Before the days of credit buying, most orders were accompanied by cold cash deposits, and the customers grew understandably annoyed when deliveries were delayed. When the first several hundred cars were finally out on the street, months late, problems turned up that careful testing would have uncovered earlier. Overheating and the quirks of the Bendix preselector gearshift quickly cooled an originally enthusiastic public. I recently heard a story, which may be true or not, of an 810 Cord with fewer than 400 miles on the odometer, sealed in a midwestern basement. It seems the original purchaser, irate over the car's tendency to boil over, literally jailed it in a fit of anger, and there it supposedly rests today.

The overheating was soon remedied, and an interlock was fitted to the Bendix gearshift to prevent chipping gears by accidentally shifting into an incorrect gear. The public remembered the early problems too well, however, and sales were hurt. A supercharged version was added in 1937, and these are the most sought-after models. The line consisted of two four-door sedans, the Beverly

Predecessor of the 810-812 series was the elegant L-29 Cord, which featured a hood nearly six feet long.

(Above) Beautiful lines of the two-passenger Sportsman. Wheelbase is 125 inches, height of the car is just 58 inches. (Below) The Lycoming V-8 produces 170 horsepower in this blown version. Note heavy bracing of the subframe, which carries engine and transmission.

Three-quarter view of the "coffin-nose" Cord. Note retractable headlamps and the cutouts in wheel covers to aid in brake-drum cooling.

Retractable headlights were positioned mechanically by hand cranks on either side of dash.

being slightly more sumptuously trimmed than the Westchester; a cabriolet; and a phaeton. Actually, the cabriolet model, designated the Sportsman, could be more accurately described as a convertible coupe. The phaeton layout was usually described by other makers, notably Packard, as a victoria.

The prices for these striking cars were surprisingly low, even for 1936. The Westchester 810 sedan listed at $1995, and the top of the line, the 810 phaeton, at $2195. All models jumped about $500 in 1937, plus an additional $400 for the supercharger, which was available on every model. Considering that the 1936 Packard Super Eight convertible victoria (Model 947) cost exactly $800 more than the 1937 supercharged 812 Phaeton, the Cord was certainly a competitive value.

Two seldom-seen models were added to the line in 1937. For those who liked more leg room, a stretched version of either sedan was available on a 132-inch wheelbase. These were listed as the Custom Beverly and the Custom Berline. The latter, at 4170 pounds, was the heaviest and most expensive model, selling for $3575.

For a car weighing close to 4000 pounds in every model, the Buehrig Cords were fast; the 1936 was capable of 92 mph, and the 1937, fitted with the Schwitzer-Cummins blower, could exceed 110 mph. Statistics for the blown engine vary, but the least boastful rates it at 170 horsepower at 4250 rpm.

Of the 2320 810s and 812s built, about half are thought to be still running. The scarce Sportsman model, like the Berline, is seldom seen at classic car meets. Mr. Adler has taken several first-place trophies with his meticulously restored convertible and has driven it to the gala Auburn-Cord-Duesenberg Club meet in Auburn, Indiana, each of the past seventeen years. Gordon Buehrig frequently attends those meets and must be deeply gratified at the devoted care hundreds of loyal owners lavish on his elegant Cord, as new today as when it left the factory thirty-six years ago.

The cleanest taillight ever designed graces the stern of Cord Sportsman.

Beautiful engine-turned dash featured full instrumentation, including a 150-mph speedometer and a tachometer. Chromed cylinder on steering column is the Bendix preselector gearshift control.

The well-designed top disappears completely under the metal hatch when not in use.

Pontoon fenders and coffin-shaped hood are most distinctive body features of the Cord.

Famed oval grille of the last series of Bugattis, the Type 57.

1937 BUGATTI TYPE 57 CONVERTIBLE COUPE

IF EVER a man lived who was to the automobile what Leonardo de Vinci was to sculpture, it was Ettore Bugatti.

Born in Milan to a brilliant and wealthy family, young Bugatti was expected to follow in his father's footsteps and become a painter or sculptor. Instead, he was entrapped by the magic of the internal-combustion engine and by his eighteenth year had actually built a respectable four-cylinder auto. Development of the self-propelled vehicle was much further advanced in Europe than in America at this time, and before 1900 Bugatti had competed in scores of races. Most of these were powered-tricycle events, with speeds around 35 mph considered extraordinary.

That first Bugatti auto earned the builder the Auto Club of France medal. It also brought the nineteen-year-old designer to the attention of Baron de Dietrich of Neiderbronn, Alsace, at that time a German province. Once lured there, Bugatti was to spend virtually all of his life in France. The baron was not put off by the tender years of his new designer, although he required Ettore's father to sign the contract for his minor son. After four years of designing and supervising the production of de Dietrich-Bugattis, Ettore was released when the plant was closed.

In the next five years Bugatti lived in the thick of the rapid-fire automotive developments occurring in Italy and France. Lancia, Isotta, and Cattaneo were his companions or opponents in the frequent races held everywhere. He was chief engineer for the Deutz Gas Engine Company briefly and designed a huge 10-liter four-cylinder engine that would be recognizable to a Bugatti buff today as the work of "Le Patron."

In 1909 he heard of a vacant dye-works complex in the town of Molsheim, Alsace. Bugatti rented the place and converted the plant into a combination auto works and estate. Early photos show solemn workers sporting mustaches lined up behind a half dozen diminutive chassis arranged on sawhorses. A half dozen was exactly the first year's production of the first genuine "pure" Bugatti.

The Model T 13 had those characteristics that would delight and astonish

Striking front view shows triple wipers on the rakish windshield.

Profile view of the clean-lined body by D'Iteren.

later generations of car lovers. Compared to the trucklike tourers that were then commonplace, the Bugatti weighed all of 660 pounds. The tread was 45 inches, and the wheelbase a subcompact 79 inches. With two passengers aboard, this sprightly machine could attain 60 mph and be run for peanuts, delivering 37 miles per gallon at 40 mph. The miniature 4-cylinder engine was cast in monobloc with a fixed cylinder head and used two vertical valves per cylinder with an overhead camshaft driven by shaft and bevel. The crankcase was an aluminum casting. Ettore's father might proudly sign his paintings; his gifted son impressed his own flowing signature on the polished surface of the cam cover of his engine creations.

Production of the highly successful T 13 increased and "Le Patron" was immediately immersed in other designs. Bugatti seems to have vacillated between large racing designs to keep in the forefront of the competition, and flawless smaller cars. The "*bebe*" was one of these low-cost, extremely simple designs, which Peugeot built under license, eventually selling over 3000.

Vestige of an aircraft fin is apparent in rear styling of this custom-bodied Bugatti.

During the war years, Bugatti had to abandon the Molsheim establishment and served the Allied cause by designing aviation engines in Paris. After the war, numerous variations of the Type 13 were built; and races were won by Bugatti every day, it seemed.

The next model to excite the racing set was the Type 35, introduced in 1924. It seems incredible, considering that Bugatti built cars only in the hundreds, that his new model would win over one thousand races and hill climbs in just two years. The Type 35 was powered by a straight eight with a five-bearing crankshaft. It displaced only 119 cubic inches. Among the car's unique features was a front axle forged with openings in it, through which the half-elliptic springs passed.

Several important racing, sporting models were made in the twenties, but several larger machines were offered for touring. The Type 44 was one of these, and the so-called baby Royale, the Type 46, was another. The Type 55 is considered one of the near-perfect Bugatti designs, capable of comfortable handling at 115 mph.

The Type 57 was again an extraordinary value (chassis price: $2860) and the most popular of all Bugattis. Between 1934 and 1939 about 750 were made. It should be remembered that the factory at Molsheim was not really a part of the contemporary industrial scene. It ran as if a guild of dedicated medieval artisans had been transferred by a time machine from Nôtre Dame Cathedral into the Molsheim grounds, with their skills converted to cope with automobile blueprints. In the entire Bugatti production span of thirty-seven years, fewer cars were made than the Chevrolet Division can assemble now in one day! Of all seventy-five or eighty model variations, the grand total built was fewer than 10,000 cars.

The beautiful convertible illustrated is a three-place drop-head coupe with a custom body by D'Iteren. This particular car was brought to the United States in 1959 and was acquired by its present owner in 1964. Restoration was limited to a new top, interior leather, and rechroming of trim. The body is of aluminum with steel fenders. An unusual feature is that the dash is not walnut or maple but pecan wood. The gas tank has a 28-gallon capacity, which gives the car a range of almost 500 miles. The eight-cylinder in-line monobloc

Pontoon effect of front fenders was popular design treatment of midthirties, as in the American Cord.

Right-hand-drive cockpit of the Bugatti.

engine is rated at 3257 cc's and produces 140 horsepower at 4500 rpm. Compression ratio is 6.2 to 1, and a one-barrel Stromberg carburetor is employed. The gear-driven double-overhead cam design is practically a Bugatti trademark. An earlier owner completely overhauled the engine, which is still performing smoothly with 71,000 kilometers on the odometer. Suspension is unusual in that quarter-elliptic springs are fitted in the rear and half-elliptics in front. This later version of the Type 57 has hydraulic brakes.

Bob Wells, a collector familiar with the driving characteristics of many classic sports cars, states that his Bugatti is remarkable in its ability to hold curves at high speed. He finds the steering light and responsive and notes that the somewhat noisy engine becomes very quiet at higher speeds. Mr. Wells has not tried to put his beautiful Bugatti to an all-out test, but with the tachometer indicating 4000 rpm at 90 mph, he is sure there is quite a bit more speed under that classic Molsheim hood.

The third passenger sat sideways, straddling the drive-train hump in this unusual seating arrangement.

The straight eight 140-horsepower engine, beautifully finished as were all Bugatti designs.

The horseshoe-shaped grille immediately identifies this graceful convertible as a Bugatti.

7. THE CONTEMPORARY SPORTING AUTO

THE term "sporting auto" may seem a strange one, but the usual appellation of "sports car" would not be correct for all the cars in this portfolio and the era under discussion. A sports car has inherent performance abilities; very high speed may or may not be one of them, but the ability to hold the road well and to handle well and securely on winding courses is paramount. A sports car has rapid acceleration through a smoothly operating manual gearbox and the braking ability to make these other qualities usable.

A car with sporting characteristics, on the other hand, may be styled like a sports car but not have the engineering design characteristics to behave like one. Immediately after World War II, interest in true sports cars mushroomed in this country. While there had always been a cult of domestic enthusiasts who lovingly tuned their BMW roadsters and vintage Bugattis, it was the growing numbers of MGs, XK Jaguars, Alfas, and other postwar European cars that developed interest in the sport here.

In the early fifties the Detroit companies decided they had better get a piece of this new action, just in case it ever became a significant part of the car-buying market. In a way that was typically American, not one major manufacturer started out to make a performance car from scratch. The small, swift, and nimble sports/touring car was really not part of the American heritage, but had sprung logically from the winding, narrow lanes of England and the twisting hairpin curves of mid-Europe's mountain roads. The American car had always been linked to the long drive across the plains and prairie country on an arrow-straight road, once an oiled gravel track and now an endless concrete ribbon. Our standards were reliability, comfort, and size, linked to the ability to pay.

The outcome of Detroit's reflections on the sports-car scene was the creation of a new automobile category; the full-size sporting, or personal car. The first of these, the 1953 Corvette, developed into a true racing machine, suited for street or track. Its first serious competitor, the 1955 Ford Thunderbird, grew from a delightful two-seater with an interesting combination of European and American traits into a four-door, four-passenger, luxury town limousine. Stude-

(Opposite) A true performer; the 1955 XK 140 MC Jaguar Roadster.

baker produced easily the most beautiful American "sports-type" of them all in 1953, designed by Raymond Loewy, who had a flair for wedding European styling to American needs of size and cost. While the basic design lasted thirteen years with a number of face-lifts, each variation moved a further step away from what had been a promising beginning. None of these Studebaker variations ever had the suspension, weight distribution, braking, or handling ability to match their sporty good looks. (The Avanti was not based on this series.)

While the personal car was being born, another domestic trend was evident: factory modification of a standard production car into a machine with sports appeal. The original 1953 Buick Skylark, the Packard Caribbean, and the Chrysler Town & Country convertibles are examples of this class. They were bold styling exercises married to the biggest engine and the swankest trim devisable. They are eminently collectible because they are very limited production models; they represent a distinct period of American auto development, and many are a pleasure to drive even two decades later. A few, such as the Kaiser Darrin, even can claim to have beauty of design.

These cars are considered in the front rank of postwar, special-interest, pseudo-sporting motorcars. The standard line of production models with lasting appeal are the convertibles, such as the 1948 to 1952 Studebakers, the pontoon-fendered Cadillacs of 1946 and 1947, and other distinctive, regular catalogue models.

The cars that follow, then, are examples of two distinctly different concepts: the cars that perform and the cars that look like performers. Each concept has a place in the hobby, and both types are being sought out and restored in increasing numbers.

(Opposite) The snug cockpit of the MG. The horn is the black button located on the dash. In lieu of a fuel gauge, a warning light flashes when gas drops below 2½ gallons.

MG is so well proportioned it belies its 94-inch wheelbase. Overall length is just 145 inches.

1952 MG MIDGET TD
TWO-SEATER

THE MG Midget sports cars belong to the British breed that was largely responsible for the rapid growth of interest in road racing in America after World War II. There were others, of course, such as the Morgan, the Singer, the Austin-Healey, and the Jaguar XK series.

The MGs had a special appeal because of their surprising performance in relation to their diminutive size. MG owners frequently capitalized on this factor, and it was common practice to lure owners of powerful, standard-size American cars into a point-to-point race. The MG driver always made sure the course included plenty of winding, hilly sections. While the big car driver was unable to unleash his superior straight-a-way speed, the MG would eat up the curves and the race.

From the early days of Morris Garages Ltd., the British company showed an interest in two-seater sportsters that could perform. The Model M of 1929 bears a surprising resemblance to the TC and TD models seen on American tracks in the fifties. A 20-horsepower, 51-cubic-inch engine gave this boattailed two-seater a top speed of 65 mph. With a fabric-covered body and cycle fenders, this nimble performer was in production until 1932. It was replaced by the J-2, which introduced the MG lines that were retained for over twenty years. The low-slung body featured cutaway doors and the familiar wedge-shaped, slab fuel tank that carried the spare wheel. The double "half-moon" dash was first used on this model. The one design feature carried over from the M model was the use of cycle fenders without running boards.

The J series carried on the successful racing tradition of the M, and a supercharged version was sold as the J3. It should be remembered that these were very light cars (1200–1300 pounds), and rather remarkable performance was being extracted from a tiny four-cylinder engine in the 750-cc range. Early victories included the Irish Grand Prix and the Ulster Tourist Trophy race.

The PB series followed the highly successful J models in 1935, and with the new sweeping fender line and running boards, their outward appearance changed little for many years. The R type followed soon after and was a giant step forward, with torsion-bar independent suspension of all four wheels. About this time, the company officially dropped out of racing, having amassed scores of first-place wins in major events in less than a decade. These wins included

Spare mounted on the external slab fuel tank was an MG trademark for years.

Profile of MG reveals that the design has the classic formula of hood length equal to half the length of the car. This well-kept example of the TD has just 48,000 miles clocked.

the Brooklands 500-mile race (twice), the Grand Prix de France, and the Tourist Trophy of Ireland. Cecil Kimber, the founder of Morris Garages (from which the MG name derives, needless to say), reportedly was weary of the constantly changing rules in handicapping the midget car class and believed that his heavy string of trophies had proved the make's qualities. After all, not every car maker could produce a car in the 750-cc class that could attain 120 mph, as the experimental MG EX127 had.

After the withdrawal from racing in 1935, MG put more emphasis on comfort and commercial sales. The TA Midget that followed no longer had the costly overhead cam engine but instead had the Morris engine with pushrod-operated overhead valves. The new model also used hydraulic brakes for the first time.

In the postwar period the MG TC was sent to America to earn badly needed dollars. (In those years immediatley after World War II, British car lovers saw new autos built and shown but not available for home purchase. Those few who were able to buy were required to pay purchase taxes equal to about one-third the value of the car.) The MG TC arrived in this country at a time when all domestic cars were in very short supply, and many Americans had a sock full of savings from war-plant wages. After a lethargic start, the MG caught on, and the demand grew rapidly. The car handled well, its 75-mph speed made it usable on the freeways, and the syncromesh gear box was forgiving of novice drivers.

When the TD was announced in 1950, many MG buffs felt that the demise of the lofty 19-inch wire wheel was a mistake. Left-hand drive and a softer suspension were among the improvements, and there is little doubt both were incorporated to appeal to the U.S. market. To serve the dedicated competitor, a Mark II TD was offered soon after, with beefed-up components giving an output of 62 horsepower and better handling.

Wire wheels were brought back in 1953 with the TF model, which was slightly longer and lower. While purists still decried the passing of the glamorous 4.50 by 19 Rudge-type, knock-off-hub wire wheels, the car admittedly was an improved performer. This model had an engine enlarged to displace 89 cubic inches. The tied-to-the-road feel was still there, and the flat, hard ride remained.

Thousands of MGs were sold in America, and most are still being driven. It seems a hard car to part with, perhaps because of the "lost-youth" syndrome. This writer has been in home garage workshops where classic car buffs have been restoring anything from a prewar Rolls to a Cadillac V-16, and frequently noted a familiar shape reposing under a tarp in the corner. One doesn't even have to lift the canvas to recognize that boxy silhouette. Commenting on the car to its owner usually releases a flood of memories and the unconvincing explanation of why the now seldom-used car hasn't been sold: "It takes no space at all, you know, might as well hold on to it."

This low-angle view emphasizes the cutaway doors and clean fender line.

Popular in the midthirties, front opening doors were considered a safety hazard in later years. Few postwar cars had them.

The TD four-cylinder produces 54 horsepower with a bore and stroke of 2.62 by 3.54 inches. Electrical system is 12 volt.

(Above) The graceful dash in MG puts the large tachometer directly before driver. Output of 54 horses was attained at 5200 rpm. (Below) Grille of 1952 MG TD.

Viewed from the front, only the cut-down windshield indicates this is not an ordinary production-line Buick.

1953 BUICK SKYLARK CONVERTIBLE

IT HAD always bothered Harlow Curtice, head of the Buick Division in the thirties and forties, that Buick could not offer limited-production or custom-bodied models. The make had climbed from fifth to third place in the industry, making five times as many cars in 1950 as the prestigious Packard. The senior series Roadmasters and Limiteds were a popular choice of doctors and bankers, and there is little doubt that limited runs of factory "specials" would have sold sufficiently to be profitable. Although the days of great wealth which supported the custom, handcrafted products of the elite shops of Brunn, Waterhouse, and Le Baron were undoubtedly over, factory customs could be produced at a fraction of the cost. One can't help visualizing a boattail-bodied Roadmaster convertible coupe on the 1938 chassis or imagining the 140-inch wheelbase Limited limousine of 1939 or 1940 as a dual-cowl phaeton. A lowered windshield, cut-down doors, and step plates instead of running boards could have changed the staid limo into an aristocratic classic.

Buick was not totally independent, of course, and as a member of the GM family probably would have been considered to be poaching on the Cadillac preserve if they had built prestige limited-run models. It is interesting to speculate on what sales effect it might have had to have a program of factory customs. Actually, Buick needed no help in the marketplace. Few cars had as steady a growth curve from 1936 through the midfifties as Buick. Packard, with unfortunate postwar styling that diffused its image, would have probably benefited from a new factory custom like the striking convertible Darrin had built on the 1940 Super Eight chassis just before the war.

Two factors led to the timing of the semicustom Skylark program: one was the Buick golden anniversary coming in 1953, the other was the replacement of the tried and true valve-in-head straight-eight engine with a new V-8 power plant. Looking over their shoulders at the fast-closing sports car crowd, Buick officials decided to market a "gentleman's sports roadster." As a sports car, the new Skylark would take the banker-owner from his suburban home to the office in exactly the same style as the standard Buicks. The difference would be largely visual, rather than in performance.

Three-quarter view of the Skylark reveals cut-down beltline, notched doors, and full rear wheel cutouts.

Starting with the Roadmaster chassis, the new convertible was lowered two inches and fitted with cut-down doors and exotic chrome wire wheels that were dramatically exposed in full fender cutouts. The sales catalogue described the car as the "Model 76-X Skylark, Two-door, Six-passenger Sports Car." Six people in a performance car seems a contradiction in terms, but was simply another way of saying Dad could have the romance of a "Jag" and still take the whole family to church in the same car.

With the exception of a rear-end continental spare wheel kit, the car was sold fully equipped. At a price approaching $5000, it was about double the cost of a standard straight-eight Buick Special.

The sleek hood housed a fine new V-8, destined to power Buicks until 1970. In its initial version, this engine displaced 322 cubic inches and developed 188 horsepower. its compression ratio was the highest in the industry at 8.5 to 1. A four-barrel downdraft carburetor was used. A new version of Buick's own Dynaflow transmission equipped with twin turbines greatly improved pickup, which had been sluggish on earlier models. Automatic transmission was standard equipment, which is probably the best single indication of how differently Detroit interpreted the term "sports car" from their European counterparts.

The Skylark was loaded with all the options offered in 1953, including a few that are no longer available. Besides the routine power brakes (supersensitive!), power steering, power seat and windows, there was the Selectronic radio, operated from a foot button that changed stations without the driver taking his hands from the wheel. Another unusual feature allowed easier access to the rear seat; when the front seatback was tipped forward, the entire front seat glided forward. Another lift to the driver's ego was provided every time he slid behind the wheel. Cast in the Lucite center medallion of the steering wheel was the original purchaser's signature.

Although the styling of the Skylark seems superficially similar to the production Roadmaster, few of the body panels are alike. The running gear is not identical either, as different universals are used. The noticeable lowering of the car's silhouette is accomplished partly by cutting down the windshied by four inches. As this six-foot, two-inch driver found, that puts the top of the windshield frame exactly at eye level. Although the genuine leather, two-tone seats are comfortable, they have been put right on the floor to ensure adequate headroom. Bumpers and headlight chrome are about all that are readily exchangeable with standard 1953 Buicks on the outside of the car. The sweeping spear that decorates the side is unique to the Skylark, as are the doorsill step plates.

Buick advertising played up the "exclusiveness" of the car and heralded the Skylark as the "originator of a new trend." It seems unlikely that GM manage-

*Lush artwork in the 1953 sales cat-
alog, which describes the Skylark
as Buick's "modern American
sports car."*

ment really thought the car would compete for those buyers who were con-
templating Jaguars or MGs. Despite the relatively low sales of the Skylark,
as well as the Packard Caribbean and the early Cadillac Eldorado, a new type
of car was created that is prospering today: the luxury, superpowerful personal
car with a sports-car aura, however faint and far removed.

I located this example of the scarce and increasingly sought-after Skylark
in Wisconsin, through a classified ad. An auto mechanic with a fondness for
Buicks of the early fifties had acquired three varied models of the make,
all with exceptionally low mileage. He had put them in storage about twelve
years earlier, but had taken pains to run the engines periodically. The body
plate indicates this Skylark to be No. 1435 of the total run of 1690 units.
The only variation from the catalogue pictured model is that the dash and
door panels are factory enameled in ivory instead of having the simulated
engine-turned veneer. New tires had been recently mounted to replace the
original wide whitewalls, which were showing sidewall cracks from age, rather
than use. A common problem that arose from long storage was the corrosion
of the contacts in the power-window lifts. Unable to raise the driver's window,
we taped a plastic drycleaner's bag in place for the 700-mile drive home
to Ohio. A quick check indicated the lights, directionals, and wipers to be
in good working order. A drive around the block revealed the brakes to be
incredibly sensitive. Lightly pumping them, however carefully, brought the
nose bobbing down on the antiquated lever shocks last used by Buick on
these 1953 models. The only technique I found satisfactory was the continuous
and delicate application of pressure on the low pedal. The 4300-pound car
responded very quickly to the brakes, even after hours of use.

With my son navigating, we soon found the Indiana turnpike and headed
home. Although all instruments indicated that everything was purring satisfac-
torily under the hood, I was somewhat apprehensive about taking a nineteen-year-old car, after a decade of dead storage, onto the turnpike for hours
of high-speed cruising. Several of the hoses were so dry as to resemble cast
iron, and shallow cracks in the radiator hose had widened appreciably by the

end of the trip. The riding qualities of the car seemed extraordinarily good. With two people in the car, and two spare doors and a few extra wheels wedged in the spacious trunk, the Skylark handled surprisingly well.

But my original intention to stay below 60 mph and favor the slow traffic lane was soon frustrated. As we neared South Bend, it began to rain, and an influx of heavy trucks forced me to maintain speed with the traffic. Coming down one long grade with a semirig ahead of me, I glanced in the tiny rearview mirror and saw an outsize rig, carrying half a prefabricated house, bearing down at flank speed. The driver apparently feared to use his brakes on the rain-swept surface and blasted his air horn instead. I found out very quickly that the twin-turbine Dynaflow could move the heavy Skylark when needed; the swift maneuver necessary to get out of the house-mover's way saw the needle briefly touch 82 mph.

The trip was otherwise uneventful, the heavy rain not penetrating the well-preserved original Orlon top. With a very weak battery that had to be jumped to start, the engine was run continuously for something over nine hours. Strangely enough, the fuel pump gave up within a few days after this demanding run and had to be replaced.

In considering the purchase of a Skylark, condition of the body and trim is paramount. Availability of parts for the engine is currently good. Running-gear parts may still be found, but interior trim, step plates, door upholstery, name plates, and the original Borrani wire wheels are really scarce. The 1954 Skylark is quite dissimilar, has a different chassis (the smaller Century model), dash, trim, and sheet metal. Only half as many of the 1954 model were made, and they are equally scarce.

As with any collected automobile, the owner of a limited-production special-interest car should constantly be alert to the spare-parts problem. Parts that are readily available now may be nonexistent in a few years. A Skylark owner, or would-be owner, would be well advised to join the Buick Club of America and thus ensure keeping abreast of current sources of parts and services.

The Skylark was advertised heavily, which helped to draw buyers to the Fiftieth Anniversary production model.

Its beauty is just the beginning

This joyous thing of exquisite grace is the Skylark— Buick's stunning new luxury sports car.

Yet the gorgeous beauty of this motorcar is just the beginning of the deep excitement.

For it's a Buick. And in any Buick, the real heart-lift you get is from the manner of its going—impeccably smooth, gentle of ride, superbly easy to handle, trigger-quick in response.

Upon the Skylark, we have lavished practically every modern automotive advance— including the world's newest V8 Engine, Twin-Turbine Dynaflow, Power Steering, Power Brakes, hydraulic control of the antenna, windows, top, and front-seat adjustment.

In other Buicks—SPECIAL, SUPER and ROADMASTER— many of these advances are yours either as standard equipment, or as options at moderate extra cost.

But in *all* Buicks—even the low-priced SPECIAL—you get the Buick Million Dollar Ride, Buick room, Buick comfort, Buick Fireball power—the highest horsepower and compression ratios, Series for Series, in all Buick history.

Your Buick dealer is waiting to seat you at the wheel of the car that will do fullest justice to your dreams and your purse. See him this week.

BUICK *Division of* GENERAL MOTORS

When better automobiles are built Buick will build them

THE GREATEST
BUICK
IN 50 GREAT YEARS

(Above) Styling of the 1953 Buick dash ran to heavy use of chrome. Power window controls were in driver's door console. (Below) The high rear wheel cutout was to display the glamorous chrome wire wheels. Rear end treatment is clean and attractive.

The original buyer's name was cast in Lucite hub emblem at the factory.

View of the crowded engine room after replacing all the hoses that dried out in 11-year layup of this low-mileage Skylark. This first V-8 Buick engine developed 188 horsepower at 4000 rpm.

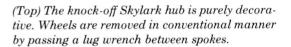

(Top) The knock-off Skylark hub is purely decorative. Wheels are removed in conventional manner by passing a lug wrench between spokes.

(Middle) Door sills are unique to the model. Little wear on this one indicates a low-mileage car.

(Bottom) All 1953 Buicks, except the lowest-price Special still powered by the venerable straight eight, wore this new hood ornament representing the V-type engine.

The sporty effect is enhanced by making the windshield and top four inches lower than the production Roadmaster Convertible.

Front view of the XK 140 MC. Introduced in 1954, the 140 series was slightly larger than the XK 120, and its engine delivered 30 additional horsepower in standard form.

1955 JAGUAR XK 140MC ROADSTER

THE ARRIVAL in America in 1949 of the first XK 120 Jaguars gave the British reputation for superior automotive quality a decided boost. The flowing lines of the aluminum-body two-seater were flawless, and under the long hood nestled a new engine destined to make racing history.

This advanced car was descended from the modest shop of an obscure builder of motorcycle sidecars; William Lyons had founded his factory in Blackpool back in 1922. The "Swallow" was an early Lyons automotive effort, using his own body design on the "Standard" chassis. That company's four-cylinder engine was used until World War II halted car production. In 1935 the Jaguar label was added to the Lyons car and designated the SS. The 1936 version of the sporty two-seater, called the SS Jaguar 100, developed an outstanding competition record and is considered one of the all-time sports car classics by collectors today.

During the war years, while the Coventry plant turned out trailers and aircraft components, Lyons and his engineering staff did much of the planning for a new postwar engine. When peace returned, these designs were finally built and tested. A slightly changed Mark V Jaguar was produced to earn cash and bridge the gap between the retirement of the old prewar Standard design and the availability of the new engine. The immensely sturdy engine that first appeared in the new X series was the end result of actually building and testing more than a half dozen designs. Its outstanding features were chain-driven, twin overhead camshafts and a hefty crankshaft carrying seven oversize main bearings. The six-cylinder engine had an aluminum head and pistons and steel connecting rods. The output of this first stock engine was 160 horsepower at 5200 rpm.

While the two-seater body of the new XK 120 was aluminum over wood and therefore light, the chassis was extremely rugged. Heavy box sections gave the frame great rigidity. The front suspension was by independent torsion bars and wide-based wishbones. Rear suspension was by conventional semielliptic springs. The large 12-inch brake drums were hydraulically operated.

The new car was a sensation at the London Auto Show in the fall of 1948.

The XK 140 with the top up. Rear wheel covers were used in conjunction with the pressed steel wheels but not with the optional wire wheels.

The Jaguar as it was most frequently seen on the competition track.

Approaching the quarter-century mark, the Jaguar body design still has a classic timeless beauty.

Early plans to devote most of the factory floor to sedan production soon had to be reevaluated. Though only 200 of the new roadsters were available, joyful owners were quickly proving the XK to be a superb performer. Production plans were changed, and bodies were made of steel on volume production lines.

Over 12,000 of the XK 120 were built, and the flood of orders required a move to a plant of almost double capacity. The wide appeal of the car resulted from that rare combination of astonishing speed, true race car handling on the level of international competition, and the pleasure every driver finds from tooling about in a beautiful machine that is delivering 20 miles per gallon of fuel. The price of approximately $4000 was substantially below other make two-seaters that could not claim half of its attributes. One of the claims that William Lyons prized particularly was that the XK 120 was the fastest production car in the world. The mark of 132.6 mph had been set with a stock XK 120 in 1949. In 1953, Lyons sent another Jaguar to the same stretch of Belgian auto route; an Austin-Healey had bettered the Jaguar record by a full 10 mph, and Jaguar Cars, Ltd., could not let the new mark stand unchallenged. The new contender was still a stock XK 120 (not the special C version that developed 210 horsepower), but fitted with the catalogue speed equipment available to the public. This included 9-to-1 ratio pistons, high-lift cams, a lighter flywheel and stiffer suspension. This XK 120 was partially streamlined by replacing the windshield with a plastic bubble and removing the bumpers. The buttoned-up Jaguar attained the incredible speed of 172 mph and regained the production car record for the now famous Coventry firm.

XKs, driven by factory teams and owner-amateurs, were winning important events everywhere, including the Silverstone Production car race, the Tourist Trophy, the Alpine Rally, and the 1951 Le Mans. In 1952, on the banked circuit at Montehery, France, an XK 120 ran continuously for an entire week, covering 16,851 miles at an average speed slightly in excess of 100 mph.

While customers waited impatiently to get their hands on these great machines, new versions were in the works. In 1954 the XK 140 was offered with the same three body styles—roadster, drop-head coupe, and closed, or fixed-head coupe. The standard engine was improved to produce 190 horsepower, and with the C-type cylinder head, that could be raised to 210. Other subtle changes gave the passengers more room, and steering was changed from recirculating ball type to rack and pinion. The car grew in weight and was now aimed more for the fast touring market than for the track. In 1958 the first wind-up windows appeared in the open-style drop head. The reliable four-speed manual gearbox could be passed over in favor of the American Borg-Warner automatic transmission if the buyer preferred. The XK 150, introduced in 1957, brought in four-wheel disc brakes. This last series carried a tail badge on the trunk lid that proclaimed in cloisonné enamel "Winner Le Mans 1951—53, 1955, 1956, 1957."

Though dressed in luxury, the larger XK 150 was the ultimate performer of the series. The S version was fitted with three carburetors, and its 265-horsepower version of the six-cylinder engine, now in its twelfth year, could move it from zero to 100 mph in 19 seconds. A top speed of 136 mph was recorded by the "Autocar" road test in an XK 150-S in 1960.

The original plans of 1948, while delayed, were not dropped, and several sedans were offered in the Jaguar line for 1950. They carried the same engine in varying degrees of output, and these cars earned a reputation as a fast, family touring machine.

The car illustrated was purchased in Indianapolis by Don Fellabaum, Jr. Condition was fair, and the new owner was able to drive the XK the 280 miles home to Ohio. After mechanical restoration, the car was repainted in ivory. Parts have presented no problem, as Jaguar distributors still service the XK series. There were some delays caused by items that had to be obtained from stocks in England. The original leather was used after being dyed. The restored roadster took first place in an all-Jaguar "Concours D'Elegance" in 1968. This model is referred to in England as the "Special Equipment" XK 140; the export version is designated the XK 140 MC. Although virtually identical in appearance to the earlier 120, the 140 is three inches longer and wider. The wheelbase of 102 inches remained the same on all XKs.

This series of true sports cars, produced in relatively large numbers, provides good hunting for the collector. Most of Jaguar's production in the fifties was sent to America to earn dollars, and the cars are still plentiful on the east and west coast. It is wise to become familiar with the variations of factory equipment, so you can more readily determine the exact model you are inspecting. Needless to say, the specially equipped models are preferred.

The MC version engine used in this XK 140 produces 210 horsepower at 5750 rpm.

Wide track and low silhouette are factors in the remarkable handling qualities of the XK series.

(Above) The attractive dash of the XK 140 features a speedometer calibrated to 140 mph. (Below) Knock-off hub of the optional wire wheels.

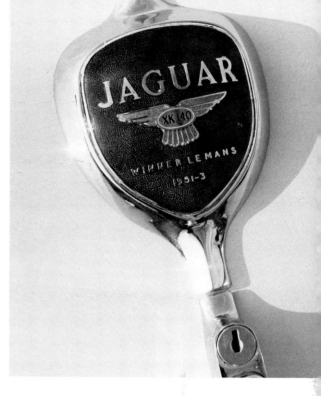

(Right) The trunk-lid tail badge notes the first two Le Mans victories. (Below) Straps on the hood are practical insurance against the hood becoming unlatched at high speed.

The porthole hardtop was a popular option offered on the 1956 and 1957 Thunderbirds.

1957 FORD THUNDERBIRD

ALTHOUGH Chrysler and Buick decided to market sports-styled cars that would be essentially modified luxury models off the production line, both Chevrolet and Ford created new cars for the postwar sports car market.

The Thunderbird existed in 1952 as a styling sketch, but it wasn't until the fall of 1954 that Ford moved to put the two-seater into production. Although sales of the new Chevy Corvette hadn't been exceptional, the public response had been enthusiastic. The appeal that the Studebaker sports coupes had had for the public wasn't lost on Ford management either.

A wise early decision was to give the buyer a choice of manual or automatic transmission. A second smart move was to provide plenty of power for a car that would be no lightweight. The 3275-pound, 175-inch long auto used the Mercury V-8 engine hotted up to produce 198 horsepower when teamed with the Ford-O-Matic drive. The stick-shift edition was mated to the 182 horsepower version. The wheelbase was set at 102 inches, and overall height was a low 52 inches. Road clearance was less than 6 inches. The Budd Company shipped complete bodies to Ford for mechanical completion, trim, and paint. The wrap-around windshield was in favor at the time, and both Corvette and the T'bird were equipped with this rather inappropriate feature for a sports car. The Thunderbird used a bench seat rather than the bucket style Corvette had elected to go with.

Purists were surprised to find an adjustable steering wheel and a four-way power seat in the Thunderbird. But the proof of Ford's judgment was soon reflected in sales—almost 14,000 sold in the first model year. This seemed to indicate that a large market existed for an American-made sports-type convertible that gave a superior ride while retaining adequate size and basic conveniences, such as crank-up windows, some trunk space, and a top that would keep out the weather. Ford was careful to include bumpers hefty enough for American parking lot maneuvers. This was one area in which European sports car designers had been notoriously weak.

The 1955 Thunderbird cost around $3500: both the Jaguar XK 140 and the Porsche Continental were in this price range. The Thunderbird did not really compete with either car, however, creating instead a new category for the car buff who wanted a solid-handling, sporty-looking car that could be serviced at the corner gas station.

Classic front end of the 1957 T'bird. Recessed, or frenched, headlights were a popular style detail of the midfifties.

(Above) Elegant engine-turned instrument panel is recessed under padded cowl. (Below) One complaint owners of the early Thunderbirds had was that steering wheel spokes blocked the view of the instruments. Note that speedometer is calibrated to 140 mph.

This *1957 Thunderbird uses the middle-sized V-8. Horsepower available ranged from 212 to a 300-horse supercharged version.*

The 1956 model was almost identical, with the optional continental rear-mounted spare the most visible addition. Vents were added to the front fenders to improve ventilation in the cockpit. The popular porthole hardtop was now available, and the engine choices included horsepower ratings of 202, 215, and 225. Over 16,000 of the 1956 models were made. For 1957, the spare was tucked inside, and up to 300 horsepower was available under the hood.

The Ford Company decided in 1958 to give the big bird four seats. The resulting car moved away from the semi-sports concept to the compact, personal luxury car. While the new Thunderbird sold well, Ford acknowledged the omission of the two-seater by introducing the Mustang in 1965. This was a car clearly based on the market lessons learned from the three classic years of the two-seater Thunderbird.

The 1957 model shown is a rare example of the car, in that it has never been restored, but has been maintained since it was new in flawless condition. Among the problems the collector faces in his search for a Thunderbird two-seater is the fact that body ventilation was not adequate, and rusting out is very common. Other Fords and the Studebakers of the period had the same problem. Finding a car from Arizona or California is one solution; another is locating new old-stock sheet metal. Unfortunately, demand for new T'bird fenders has depleted stocks, and most cars found will show signs of body-shop patching. Given a choice between a smoothly purring engine and a rust-free body, most collectors will choose the two-seater Thunderbird with a solid body. While a sound example of the original design is becoming relatively scarce and expensive, interest is developing in the early 1958–62 four-seaters. These are plentiful and at very reasonable prices.

Continental rear wheel kit was offered on the 1956 Thunderbird.

Massive new bumpers and distinctive louvered wheel covers marked the 1957 T'bird. This immaculate example has been driven less than 45,000 miles.

A clean rear deck and dual exhausts incorporated in the dramatic new rear bumper set the 1957 model apart from earlier versions.

Dual headlights and heavier grille first appeared on the 1958 Corvette and were unchanged through this 1960 model.

1960 CHEVROLET CORVETTE

THE Corvette originated in that period of the early fifties when domestic car makers had finally brought their production to a level adequate to meet the pent-up demand of almost five auto-less war years. With full coffers they could now study the national scene and see if any marketing bets were being overlooked.

Even a cursory glance at the nearest parking lot revealed something that hadn't been there before the war—little cars, and in growing numbers. Oddball little cars like the Jeepster, the Crosley, and a few Nash-Healeys. Even more evident was the growing number of pert little English MG sports cars, almost always wearing "British Racing Green." There were many sleek XK Jags, and a sprinkling of Alpha-Romeos and Ferraris as well.

Harley Earl, the General Motors styling chief, had noted this trend and pushed for a Chevy product to compete with these popular new imports. It is interesting to see how each company met that fork in the road; one fork leading to true performance, the other to mere sporty window dressing. An examination of the Corvette history reveals that credit for the true sports machine that evolved must be divided between the company and those first buyers. Perhaps the buyers expected more than they got in the 1953–54 version. The car was a compromise: a sleek, sporty, classic body with a relatively high-performance six-cylinder engine of 235-cubic-inch displacement. With this was a slightly modified Chevy sedan suspension, solid axles, and incredibly enough, two-speed Powerglide. It would seem that this "dual-purpose" sports-type car would attract neither the road and track buff nor the banker's hot-rod gentry. While Chevrolet was vacillating between making an American XK out of the Corvette, or a Buick Skylark, those first customers became very vocal. The car was raced, and in events like the Palm Springs Road Race of 1955 could not cope with the MGs. A distinguished American driver, John Fitch, entered a team of Corvettes at Sebring in 1956 and 1957. His suggestions, as well as advice from hundreds of others who had fallen for the "Vette," poured into Chevrolet. The company listened, tested, changed, and tested again. No conscious decision was made, but the car was now headed for the status of the one pure road/track sports car made in America.

Fewer than 4000 of the white fiberglass-bodied cars were made in 1953 and 1954. The really scarce Corvette is the 1955 model, with a production run of 700, all with the 265-cubic-inch V-8, and most still equipped with Powerglide.

The principal difference between the classic body of this 1960 Corvette and earlier 1956 and 1957 models is the addition of wraparound rear bumper and front fender vent.

The Corvette cockpit is a successful combination of American production car luxury and European sports car practicality and comfort.

1960 Corvette retains its clean lines with the soft top up. This show specimen has traveled just 19,000 miles in twelve years.

The 1956 models saw improvements in both racing capability and comfort. The top and windows could be had with power options, a detachable hardtop was available, and the dash and cockpit were made more stylish. Performance was helped by better suspension, a close-ratio three-speed gearbox, and a choice of engine versions. The 225-horsepower, middle-sized V-8 allowed an astonishing 108 mph in second gear. The 240-horsepower engine, with a high lift cam, was theoretically capable of moving the 1956 Vette to the 130 mph range.

Rochester fuel injection was added to an enlarged V-8 in 1957. Even though the weight of the car had been inching up (now 2840 pounds), the 283 horses available was more than sufficient to improve the breed still further. With an all-syncromesh four-speed transmission, the fuel-injected Corvette had finally arrived as a truly potent track contender. Proof of this was soon demonstrated by wins over the prestigious Mercedes 300 SL in production car class events.

In a situation that is somewhat reminiscent of what happened when styling changes were made in the postwar Lincoln Continental (after the clean-lined original), some purists scorn every Vette made from 1958 on. Quad headlights were introduced, as well as a massive new grille and bumper. The silhouette of the car was unchanged, but an arty air scoop was added to the front fender and wraparound bumpers to the rear. As a matter of personal taste, this writer finds all Vettes esthetically pleasing, including the 1958 through 1962. The 1963–67 series is really a different automobile in its styling, as are the 1968 and newer models.

The 1960 model illustrated is the last one having the original design profile; the 1961 model introduced the upturned tail which preceded the Stingray model. Optional aluminum heads were available in 1960 to raise horsepower to 315, and subtle changes were made in the suspension, including bigger antiroll bars and improved handling. Since 1958, production had been stabilized at around 10,000 units a year. Exactly 10,261 of the 1960 model pictured were made.

The Stingray styling of 1963, probably the most advanced design of the year

Not the most accessible engine room. The 283-cubic-inch Chevy V-8 engine, including fuel injection, was standard in a number of versions from 1957 to 1961. Output ranged from 200 horsepower in 1957 to 315 in the hottest 1961 engine.

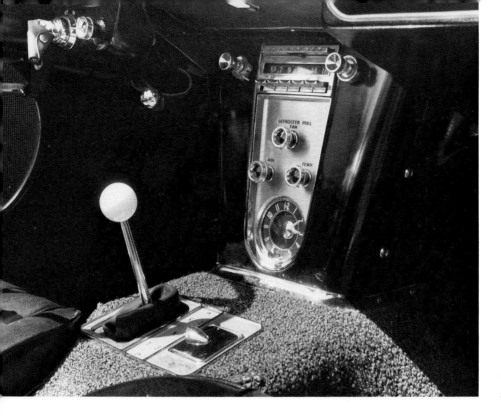

The console houses ventilation controls, radio, and clock.

(with the possible exception of Loewy's Avanti for Studebaker), drew buyers in increasing numbers. Over 21,000 were sold.

Each succeeding Corvette managed to attain higher levels of acceleration and speed. In 1966, car buffs must have murmured, "When will it all end?" That year's stock Vette, with an immense 427-cubic-inch engine rated at 425 horsepower, could attain 140 mph in just 17 seconds!

At least one competitor has driven his Corvette to Sebring, run the 12-hour event, and driven his entry 1000 miles home. Perhaps that is symbolic of how well the Chevrolet Division of General Motors succeeded in creating a sports car suited for both road and track. The success of the Corvette program should provide collectors with cars for years to come. Over 14,000 of the "classic" period models were made between 1953 and 1957, and about a quarter million more Vettes from 1958 to the present.

Some purists prefer a fender line without elaborate vent fins, first seen on the 1958 model Corvette.

Front-end styling of the 1960 Corvette.

Striking front end of the Avanti is not just style. Tests proved air intake below bumper level to be more efficient; hence there is no need for conventional open grille.

1963 STUDEBAKER AVANTI

THE Studebaker story goes back long before autos existed. Abe Lincoln, at forty-three, was not yet a nationally known figure when Henry and Clem Studebaker sold their first wagon in 1852. Brother John came back from the California gold rush a few years later and staked the family wagon-builders to an expanded shop in South Bend, Indiana. The firm was soon a giant in its field and by 1900 was the biggest maker of wagons and carriages in the world. With a loyal following of more farmers than any other builder of wheeled goods could claim, Studebaker had an early advantage when the auto age dawned.

When the company turned to cars, they first dabbled in electrics, then had other firms make cars for Studebaker to distribute. By the twenties Studebaker had a sound reputation as the sixth- or seventh-place American car. Their big six was a fast and dependable trend setter. Sales were so good, Studebaker enjoyed the largest percentage growth of any American auto maker. Record making and record breaking was the big promotion device of the roaring twenties, and Studebaker earned their share of prizes. A six-cylinder Commander sped coast to coast in seventy-seven hours in September of 1927. A month later three stock sedans completed the grueling feat of running 25,000 miles in under 25,000 minutes. The company won domestic races, and Studebakers popped up in the winner's circle from Hamburg, Germany, to Rio de Janeiro, Brazil.

In 1928, when the President Eight was introduced, every closed-sedan, stock-car record fell to the new car. Stutz had tangled with Hispano-Suiza and the "Bentley Boys," but it is little known that Studebaker sent a team entry to the Brooklands Motor Speedway for an international event in 1928. In an incredible test of endurance over a 1700-mile course, the Presidents won the race with an average speed of 71 mph. The list of the competitors that failed to finish, blew up, or trailed badly reads like a who's who of European racing classics: Bentleys, Bugattis, Lagondas, Alfa-Romeos, and Frazer-Nashes, among others. A British journalist noted: "The Studebakers, which, after all, are not even speed or sport models came over the line as fresh as when they began. They had run most impressively without any fireworks, and yet had averaged over 70 mph."

(Above) Totally instrumented with fourteen
gauges, the Avanti dash is a model of functional
design. (Right) The steering wheel is designed
to provide unobstructed view of dash. Speedometer is calibrated to 160 mph.

(Opposite) The angle of rounded wedge shape is evident in this three-quarter rear
view of the Avanti. Hatch giving inside access to the trunk may be seen behind
rear seat.

The rear seat accommodates two passengers in semi-bucket comfort. Note the padded roll bar.

Although the engineers and designers at South Bend had proved their product could compete with any car in their price range (and with many more expensive cars), management decisions hastened the difficult days ahead when the stock market would collapse. Sales in 1928 reached $177 million, and enormous dividends were paid to stockholders in 1929. But the crash came just after Studebaker had bought a controlling interest in the ailing Pierce-Arrow Company. With the company now tied to cars in the upper price range, and working capital at a low level out of proportion to their recent heavy earnings, Studebaker turned to the track once more. Modified President "Specials" did well in the Indy 500 of 1932, and one driven by Cliff Bergere finished third. In 1933 six basically stock Presidents were entered and all six finished, taking sixth to twelfth place, a record no other production car ever approached.

Racing couldn't help sales, however, and naming a new $600 car after America's favorite football coach couldn't make a success of the low-priced Rockne. The crash had finished any dream of making Pierce a counterpart of Henry Ford's Lincoln, and Studebaker sold that distinguished relic of the past in 1933 at a loss. Studebaker went into receivership, and a few months later their president, Albert Erskine, shot himself. Even in the depression, however, Studebaker had such a strong reputation that it finally weathered the storm. Paul Hoffman led the company out of receivership, and among his smartest moves was hiring Raymond Loewy to style future Studebakers.

Just when the new, crisply modern Champion was selling well, Europe went up in flames and auto production ceased. The ensuing war years gave the firm a breather, time to assess what place Studebaker should seek in the postwar auto market. Between 1941 and 1945 the plant hummed with war production;

more than a quarter million heavy trucks were built, most of which saw lend-lease service on the Russian front. Like Packard, Studebaker ended war production in great shape. Unlike Packard, or anyone else in Detroit for that matter, Studebaker had done their homework, and showing more vision and courage than they had since the President days of 1928, launched a dazzling new automobile.

"Is it coming or is it going?" became a national wisecrack. It was an admiring and affectionate remark, however, and the dramatically different car became the sales success of South Bend. The slab-sided car with the long rear deck and short hood was continued until 1952. The 1949 edition sold over 200,000 units in three lines: Champion, Commander, and Landcruiser.

Typical of Studebaker management, unfortunately, was the fiasco that occurred in 1953 with the daring new Loewy-designed coupe. The car was an instant success in the salesroom when shown in late 1952, but, as has happened before, notably to Cord, a car was promoted that wasn't ready for delivery. Stubborn "brass" at Studebaker still considered the family sedan the keystone of the catalogue, and most of the tooling money had gone for sedan production, based on a ratio of four sedans to one sport coupe. They had further tampered with Loewy's sedan design and made it a conventional and stodgy partner to the sleek coupe and hardtop. They also refused to build any convertibles, when that style was in growing demand.

In 1954 came the merger with Packard. It was extraordinary that only five years after their successful postwar peak, both of these landmark companies would be in major trouble. In retrospect it would seem that Studebaker tried

The center console features the Powershift lever. Option of manual or automatic gear-changing was unique with the Avanti at the time.

The modified 289-cubic-inch Studebaker V-8 uses a high lift cam, has a 9 to 1 compression ratio, and is equipped with Paxton supercharger, delivering 280 horsepower at 4800 rpm.

to compete with General Motors too much in marketing a full line of cars. The company went downhill steadily until President Harold Churchill earned a brief respite with the timely Lark in 1959. This attractive compact was ingeniously cobbled out of tooling that dated back to 1954. Despite his success, Churchill could not get the money he wanted to style a really new compact to stay ahead of Detroit, and he was replaced by Sherwood Egbert in 1961.

The Avanti story starts with Egbert and his appreciation of what Raymond Loewy might once again do to pull Studebaker back from the abyss. Although legend has it that Egbert sketched the new car profile on the back of an envelope, the Avanti is strikingly similar to several "one-off" idea cars Loewy had commissioned in Italy earlier, notably a 1960 Lancia. Much has been made of the fact that the Avanti was conceived in something like forty days. While Loewy had been out of Studebaker affairs since 1956, he had been leisurely developing his ideas for a Gran Turismo machine on several European chassis, including the BMW and Jaguar, as well as the Lancia.

The development of the Avanti went ahead in the cloak-and-dagger secrecy of a rented house in Palm Springs, California. Both Egbert and Loewy were decisive men with respect for one another. Management support was no doubt helped by the sales record of those earlier Studebakers created by Loewy in 1939, 1947, and 1953. The venerable chassis of 1953, in the beefed-up form used by the 1961 Lark Daytona convertible, was to be the platform for this new

No conventional Studebaker body hardware was employed on Avanti. Door handles were flush mounted to provide the smoothest surface possible.

grand touring car. The reliable Hawk 289-cubic-inch V-8 engine was selected as the power plant. Modifications brought this engine to an honest 225 horsepower, and a blown version, using the Paxton Supercharger, raised this to 280 horsepower.

The wedge-shaped body was designed to achieve stability at high speeds. Coupled to the lightweight fiberglass shell was a chassis equipped with disc brakes up front and big drums at the rear. Among the unique features incorporated was an integral roll bar, a tube of high-tensile-strength steel upholstered to match the headliner. Several instruments were located in an overhead panel, as on a plane. Safety-cone door locks virtually sealed the doors against the possibility of accidently opening.

The new Powershift transmission gave the driver some of the freedom of manual selection of gears in a fully automatic transmission, if desired. Although giving the impression of a lean and taut design on the outside, the Avanti interior was planned for four adults to ride in comfort.

While the Studebaker production people were struggling with plastic body problems, Andy Granatelli took three of the new cars to the Bonneville Salt Flats and proceeded to demolish every record in sight. With the R-3 engine, certified as 299.4 cubic inches, and the Paxton blower at work, the Avanti ran the stock car flying mile at 168.15 mph. A dozen records were broken, many of them only recently set by a Pontiac of at least 100 additional horsepower.

Egbert soon realized that the 1962 production goal of 20,000 cars could never be met if they depended on an outside body builder. Studebaker thereupon built their own fiberglass body plant. With such a car as the Avanti, it seems incredible that many of the directors at that time wanted to drop all auto production. In December of 1963, with large stocks of slow-selling 1964 Larks on hand, Studebaker announced the move to Canada, a way station to oblivion. Not even the Avanti records and buyer response could prompt the company

The wedge-shaped theme is carried through to the wheel cover design.

Turn signals are sunk into knife-edge fenders. The easiest identification difference between 1963 and 1964 Avanti is the headlights; in 1964, lights were mounted in a square frame.

to take what seemed the most logical step; namely, drop everything but production of the Hawk and Avanti lines. By standardizing on the Paxton-equipped V-8, Studebaker might have continued the Hawk as the convertible it should have been in the first place. The government had offered military truck contracts that could have helped avert mass layoffs in South Bend, providing time needed to smooth out volume production of the Avanti.

There is little doubt the Avanti was worth the $4200 price. The proof of the market is the Corvette sales record, currently running at 30,000 plus per year. The Avanti was probably the most successful family-sized (four passengers plus luggage) grand touring machine ever made in postwar America. Its demise is mourned by car buffs who wouldn't look at any other Studebaker.

A trickle of refined editions is still being lovingly assembled by former Studebaker craftsmen in South Bend. The successor company (Avanti Motor Corporation), a decade later, still thinks they have the newest shape on the automotive scene, and they may be right.

Only the tiny plate on left fender identifies supercharged model from standard version.

Overall length of the Avanti is 192 inches on a wheelbase of 109 inches.

Lightweight fiberglass body 54 inches high and 70 inches wide contributes to low center of gravity and excellent handling.

AUTOMOBILE CLUBS

The number of old car clubs has been increasing rapidly, with the recent emphasis on clubs of one make.

The long-established major clubs include the following:

The Antique Automobile Club of America, Inc., West Derry Road, Hershey, Pa. 17033

The Classic Car Club of America, P.O. Box 443, Madison, N.J. 07940

Horseless Carriage Club of America, 9031 East Florence Avenue, Downey, Calif. 90240

The Veteran Motor Car Club of America, 15 Newton Street, Brookline, Mass. 02146

Recent national clubs devoted to the special-interest auto include:

The Contemporary Historical Vehicle Association, Inc., 71 Lucky Road, Severn, Md. 21144

The Milestone Car Society, Room 505, 85 East Gay Street, Columbus, Ohio 43215

Notable among the one-make clubs are the following:

The Buick Club of America, P.O. Box 853, Garden Grove, Calif. 92642

Cadillac LaSalle Club, 30670 Kirk Lane, Franklin, Mich. 48025

Lincoln Zephyr Owners' Club, Fran Olweiler, Box 185, Middletown, Pa. 17057

Kaiser-Frazer Owners' Club International, Mrs. M. Ehlers, Sec., 4015 South Forest, Independence, Mo. 64052

The Studebaker Drivers Club, Inc., P.O. Box 3044, South Bend, Ind. 46619

Packards International, P.O. Box 1347, Costa Mesa, Calif. 92626

Model A Restorers Club, P.O. Box 1930A Dept. H, Dearborn, Mich. 48121

Model A Ford Club of America, P.O. Box 2564, Pomona, Calif. 91766

Auburn, Cord, Duesenberg Owners' Club, Box 147, Milpitas, Calif. 95035

Lincoln Continental Owners' Club, National Headquarters, 28 Harmony Lane, Westbury, N.Y.

There are literally scores of clubs for other makes, as well as for electrics and steamers. The club-event columns of the hobby publications will indicate which clubs are active in the reader's area.

AUTOMOBILE MUSEUMS

It is advisable to find out the schedule of visiting hours and days open before traveling to any museum. This selection of museums is listed according to geographical location, east to west.

Museum of Transportation, Larz Anderson Park, Brookline, Mass. 02146
Long Island Automotive Museum, Southampton, N.Y.
Ellenville Motor Museum, Ellenville, N.Y.
Smithsonian Institution, Transportation Division, Washington, D.C.
Gene Zimmerman's Automobilorama, U.S. 15 at Penn. Turnpike near Harrisburg, Pa.
Bellm Cars and Music of Yesterday, U.S. 41, Sarasota, Fla.
Frederick C. Crawford Auto-Aviation Museum, Western Reserve Historical Society, 10825 East Boulevard, Cleveland, Ohio 44106
Henry Ford Museum and Greenfield Village, Dearborn, Mich.
Indianapolis Motor Speedway Museum, 4790 West 16th Street, Speedway, Ind. 46224
Brooks Stevens Automotive Museum, Route 141, Mequon, Wis.
Museum of Science and Industry, Chicago, Ill.
The Museum of Automobiles, Petit Jean Mountain, Ark.
Harrah's Auto Collection, Reno, Nev.
The Classic-Car Showcase, Houston, Tex.
Briggs Cunningham Automotive Museum, 250 Baker Street, Costa Mesa, Calif.

Any car buff traveling in Europe should inquire locally about nearby auto museums, because dozens of outstanding collections are open to the public in many countries. We call attention to the Daimler-Benz Museum in Stuttgart, West Germany; the Lourdes Automobile Museum in that French city; and the beautifully housed collection in Turin, Italy, the Museo dell-Automobile Carlo Biscaretti di Ruffia.

AUTOMOTIVE LIBRARIES

Information on old automobiles can be obtained from these libraries. Charges vary, but are usually based on an hourly rate for the librarian's time plus the cost of the necessary photostats. The major automotive libraries are:

Automotive History Collection, Detroit Public Library, 5201 Woodward Avenue, Detroit, Mich.
Frederick Crawford Auto-Aviation Museum, Western Reserve Historical Society, 10825 East Boulevard, Cleveland, Ohio
The Ford Archives, Henry Ford Museum, Dearborn, Mich.
Long Island Automotive Research, Meadow Spring, Glen Cove, N.Y.
Thomas McKean Collection of the Automobile, Free Library of Philadelphia, Logan Square, Philadelphia, Pa.

SELECTED BIBLIOGRAPHY

Bentley, W.O. *The Cars in My Life.* New York: Macmillan Co., 1963.
Borgeson, Griffith, and Jaderquist, Eugene. *Sports and Classic Cars.* New York: Prentice-Hall, 1955.
Buckley, J.R. *Cars of the Connoisseur.* New York: Macmillan Co., 1962.
Georgano, G.N. *The Complete Encyclopedia of Motorcars.* New York: E.P. Dutton & Co., 1969.
Helck, Peter. *The Checkered Flag.* New York: Charles Scribner's Sons, 1961.
Hough, Richard, and Frostick, Michael. *A History of the World's Classic Cars.* New York: Harper & Row, 1963.
Maxim, Hiram P. *Horseless Carriage Days.* New York: Harper & Brothers, 1937.
Scott-Moncrief, David. *Classic Cars 1930-1940.* Cambridge, Mass.: Robert Bentley, Inc. 1963.
Turnquist, Robert E. *The Packard Story.* New York: A.S. Barnes, 1966.

PERIODICALS

Hobby publications run the gamut from newsprint classified-ad monthlies to the elegant, hardbound, four-color *Automobile Quarterly*. All serve a vital role in pursuing the old-car hobby. They provide information impossible to obtain through normal library channels. In their pages may be found innumerable sources of cars, parts, and tires, as well as vital owners and shop manuals. They also enable owners to exhange their experiences in solving many restoration problems. A few of these publications are:

Automobile Quarterly, 245 West Main Street, Kutztown, Pa. 19530
Car Tips Magazine, Box 11, Babylon, N.Y. 11702
Cars & Parts, P.O. Box 299, 144 East Franklin Avenue, Sessor, Ill. 62884
Car Classics, Iola, Wis. 54945
Hemmings Motor News, Box 380, Bennington, Vt. 05201
Old Cars, Iola, Wis. 54945
Special Interest Autos, Box 196, Bennington, Vt. 05201

Many other outstanding publications are produced by the major clubs, and membership in a club includes a subscription to their quarterly.

INDEX